GIVE YOURSELF A RAISE:

Common Sense Principles to Help You
Think, Act and Live More Abundantly

TRAVIS YOUNG

ACTIVE EDIT

PUBLISHING

NEW YORK, NEW YORK

Publisher's Cataloging in Publication
(Prepared by Quality Books Inc.)

Young, Travis.
      Give yourself a raise : common sense principles to help you think, act and live more abundantly / Travis Young.
        p. cm.
        LCCN: 95-96058
        ISBN 0-9650566-1-9

      1. Self-actualization. 2. Career development. 3. Success 4. Finance, Personal.   I. Title

BF637.S4Y68   1996   158'.1
                      QBI96-20178

This book is printed on recycled, acid-free paper.

DEDICATION

*For my parents, who were raised in very difficult
environments and have grown despite great obstacles,*

and

*For my nieces
(Heather, Jennifer, Lacey, Cassie, Katie, Danielle, Kelsie,
Taylor, and Rebecca) and my nephews (Josh and Tyler),
who are an abundant source of joy
and ever remind me of life's most precious gifts*

ACKNOWLEDGMENTS

Holly Ohren, for her support, patience and loyalty.

Allen Ascher, for his positive input, writing expertise, and publishing suggestions.

Richard Holt, Michael Toles, Augie Hasho, and **Joseph Barbaccia**, whose encouragement helped me to keep going on this project.

Carol Quatrone and **Larry Dvoskin**, who offered their guidance in helping me plan this book.

David Moshier, Jan Nathan, Barbara Graham, and **Rodney Charles**, who shared their time and experience freely.

Steve Young and **Mark Young**, my brothers, and **Terri Swaggerty** and **Barbara Armstrong**, my sisters, and all of their spouses; and my friends and my clients, all of whom have enriched my experience of life.

Copy Editing by: Allen Ascher
New York, New York

Cover Design &   Rai and Beth Richardson
Book Layout by: Springfield, Illinois

TABLE OF CONTENTS

PREFACE

This material has evolved from my work with men and women who have come to me seeking alternatives, new directions, and new opportunities for financial, professional and personal growth. So much progress has been made by such a wide variety of individual clients, from different walks of life, it became evident that it would be a service to share some of these principles with others.

The following pages contain suggestions, ideas, and concepts that I practice myself and pass along, to the best of my ability, to my clients. Many ideas are repeated and overlap in different chapters. This is intentional and demonstrates that the principles need continual reinforcement and work in harmony with one another.

You do not have to practice everything written here to derive positive benefits. Use as many of these ideas as you can that make sense to you. The way these suggestions are presented here does not matter as much as what you take from them.

Take as much time as you need to go through the material. Do not try to integrate everything at once. For some individuals, provocative feelings and emotions may arise from confronting long-held beliefs that make it even more important to proceed gently, not plow ahead.

Do not give up on the desire to find and practice principles of self-care and inner-fulfillment that led you to pick up and read this book. I hope the experiences and ideas discussed in this material can be helpful to you. If you only get a single idea that helps you better understand how to improve your financial, professional or personal circumstances, this book has served its purpose.

Travis Young

SECTION I
GET READY TO RAISE THE LEVEL OF YOUR PROSPERITY

Genuinely considering new thoughts and ideas is the beginning of all accomplishment. It is the foundation for all of mankind's achievement. It is the basis for personal fulfillment and satisfaction.

For our purposes, to get ready to raise your level of prosperity you begin by simply reading this material and relating the overall principles and suggestions to your own situation. This is considering new thoughts and ideas.

Hopefully, many of the ideas you will read about will seem like good common sense, maybe even things you already knew. So much the better. If this is so, it may be easier for you to try using them. These concepts may, however, be "new" in the sense that you have not specifically thought about them or how you may put them to use in you life. This book will help motivate you to do so.

There is nothing in this book "too simple to work" or so complicated you cannot "get it" if you take some time to examine these ideas. In the discussion of these concepts, many factors will be touched upon, including practical, psychological, emotional, even physical and spiritual issues. You are a holistic being -- meaning all aspects of your life affect one another. If you are to live more abundantly, this book needs to address your overall well-being and factors that impact upon it. For example, what good would it do you to increase your income while you are having greater stress and no time to enjoy life?

Conversely, it would not be helpful if you were motivated to find more meaningful work and could not pay your bills or maintain your health. The aim of the principles discussed here is toward success **and** satisfaction **and** balance.

The first thing to do to raise the level of your prosperity is simply to stimulate your thinking. Getting ready is an action of the mind.

Is Abundance for You?

*I spent everything I had to keep myself
from having anything.*
A former client

With rare exception, we are born as naturally abundant creatures. We possess the ability to learn, adapt and flourish in the environment around us. However, as children, many of us were raised under harsh circumstances or with frightened, angry adults. Environments such as these can effectively short circuit our natural inclinations to explore, grow, and thrive. As a result, many of us become experts at survival, but it is just survival. Often, too much of our existence turns into a struggle. We continue to reinforce the state of adversity in which we originally lived. It is unfortunate that many of us received training that taught us to deny ourselves. Internalized mechanisms of self-deprivation are at the root of why we do not enjoy life's gifts to a much greater degree. We can want so much more, strive and strain, and yet prosperity and greater abundance elude us. As long as these negative internalized mechanisms go undetected, we can keep ourselves from moving ahead and raising the level of our prosperity.

Many of us keep ourselves from having a great deal of life's rewards. A career that is satisfying and pays well and more satisfying personal and professional relationships are things we often want and do not obtain. We can come to think we lack the skills or knowledge others seem to possess. We can also avoid taking care of ourselves with vacations and time off, enjoying quality possessions, seeking proper health treatment and acquiring better homes, etc. Often though, deprivation shows up in small ways. For example, we deprive ourselves of abundant living by refusing to spend a few extra dollars on taking a cab, getting popcorn at the movies, buying a few gourmet food items, paying for name brands, and purchasing supplies conveniently, instead of shopping in crowded, chaotic, out of the way stores where we "save" money. Alternately, we can constantly spend too much on "treats we deserve for the things we put up with" and never have enough money to improve the substance of our lives.

We also deprive ourselves by leaving too little time to address our needs. By spending just a few minutes on non-essential tasks or by delaying ourselves a short time, we can find ourselves rushing to beat the clock and become anxious getting to work, making an appointment, or getting to the bank, post-office or store before closing. Some of us also deprive ourselves by being excessively responsible to others. We do this even when we need to say "No" for our own well-being. Often out of a false sense of obligation, we do errands, stay on the phone, listen endlessly, clean up after someone, and otherwise help others even when it deprives us (and robs them of learning how to care for themselves). In this way we deprive ourselves of time we need to rest, relax, or do something pleasurable that replenishes us. In dozens of little ways, we deny ourselves and virtually remain in stress -- living on the edge.

If we continue to deprive ourselves, we can feel alone no matter how many people are in our lives. In a sense, we are alone, *in our fear, confusion, and frustration,* wondering what it is we need to solve our pressing problems or get ahead in our lives. Other people make progress and seemingly leave us behind. In truth, we learned to leave ourselves behind.

Some of us may have overcome much of our self-depriving behavior or were lucky enough to have gotten a better head start. This does not make us immune to yearnings or painful feelings. We can still feel deprived in a particular area of our lives. If we do, it is easy to fall into the trap of magical (unrealistic) thinking. The illusion is that the "right" actions will provide us with more money and better circumstances or, in achieving a certain goal, we will be happy and secure. It is common wisdom that what we "possess" cannot give us the internal security we truly need to adjust to life's challenges and enjoy life's gifts. Though money is important for us all, prosperity and abundance mean far more than financial well-being. Prosperity and abundance are words often used interchangeably and are defined using phrases such as ample and plentiful, flourishing, and thriving. Assuming this is true, prosperity and abundance are a great deal more than simple monetary comfort. Abundant living, then, is marked by a philosophy of well-being in which we experience our lives as plentiful and flourishing. We carry the internal knowledge that we can care for ourselves thoughtfully and lovingly, regardless of how our external (and financial) environment changes. To put it another way, prosperous and abundant living needs to include an overall sense of satisfaction, stimulation and contentment along with feelings of capability and self-respect. This means we can experience ourselves as flourishing and thriving even when we face difficult challenges, make mistakes, and operate with a host of human imperfections.

These images evoked by the words prosperity and abundance expand the idea of success. At the turn of the century, success was not limited to those who had material wealth or celebrity. In fact, many of those individuals were held in great disdain by fellow citizens. In our society's past, a person was thought successful if he or she was hard working, of good character, committed, loyal, and of service to family and community. In this society, we have largely abandoned these criteria of success in favor of financial accumulation and media fame. In the ideas proposed above, we might consider adding the idea that true success is also marked by inner satisfaction and a positive experience of our overall existence. In this event, positive principles of living are equally important as relative financial comfort and professional influence. Money and stature cannot then be our only goals if we are to increase our sense of contentment, peace and healthy personal pride. This means that focusing on external goals alone to attain abundance and prosperity is an illusion which finally results in mediocre or painful living.

We need to shift our beliefs and attitudes and work to change our philosophy. If we do not expand our idea of success, we can find ourselves depressed after accumulating more material wealth. Gaining recognition or winning awards will not keep us from internal deprivation and emotional hardship. We may achieve a dream and then feel lost, or become successful in a career and find out later that we do not like it. Therefore, raising the level of our abundance operating under old, self-defeating, self-depriving, and image-driven philosophies is not possible.

If these old mechanisms are in place, we may have a deeply embedded belief that a contented life is beyond our grasp. If we "fail" to reach important goals, we may feel joyless, bored and painfully empty. If we learned to deny ourselves and/or focus only on external solutions to our problems, we suffer. Enduring much frustration, we see ourselves as victims of circumstance with a belief that we are inadequate to do anything about it.

Despite these negative experiences, there is hope. Something inside us suspects we can be much more fulfilled. We sense that we can learn to adopt new ways of thinking and acting which make a more rewarding professional and personal life possible That is why we pick up books like this one. We do not wish to let go of that expressive and self-caring spirit given to us at birth.

It is probable that you have picked up this book to explore, in some measure, how you might be more contented in your life. If this is so, you have taken a wonderful action based on the idea that greater abundance is for you. You have raised this desire and have taken a step toward fulfilling it.

When the Going Gets Tough

CHAPTER 2

> *Suffering is a divine gift in disguise.*
> Confucius

Discontentment, frustration, anger, fear, anxiety, confusion, emptiness, yearning -- these are not fun feelings. They can, however, serve useful purposes. Our feelings and inner experiences are messages to us. They are trying to tell us something the same way a toothache tells us to visit the dentist or take better care of our teeth.

If certain distressing feelings and inner experiences persist, especially in a particular area of our lives, we know we need to change something. We may not know what to change or how to change it, but changing seems extremely important lest we continue to suffer distress by ignoring the messages. If we ignore what we know, life has a way of creating circumstances that may force us to deal with the messages we are avoiding (i.e., getting fired, losing a relationship, others passing us by, financial crisis, intense physical or emotional pain). If you are one among us who needs to listen to internal messages telling us to "wake-up and do something," you are in the right place to read on.

Time to Get Going

I have yet to meet a person who has not felt like they should have addressed some of their problems sooner. Despite the philosophy that we each evolve exactly in the time frame that is needed, it is common to believe we have wasted time or procrastinated. There is truth to both ideas. We are where we need to be, and we also procrastinate and waste time. Nevertheless, the more important questions are: How do you feel about your circumstances today? Are you prepared to do something different about your situation? Do you understand things will not change unless you do something different to help yourself? Are you willing to try new things even if they may not work? It is your answers to these questions that determine your readiness to have more prosperity and abundance in your life.

If you are not ready to do anything different right now about having more prosperity, so be it. Accept that for now. Do not criticize yourself if you need more time. Reading these ideas is enough for the moment. There were periods in my life when I could only vaguely consider changing the way I operated. I was not yet ready. By this point in my life, however, I have learned not to wait too long to take action. My feelings and inner experiences tell me something and I do not wait for months or years, as before, to start the process of change. This can be the case for any of us who wish it so.

It is time we all get going. What are we waiting for? We can begin today to entertain a new thought, act on a new idea, listen to and express our dreams and goals. Greater abundance and prosperity are awaiting us like flowers in a field waiting to be picked. It is we who keep ourselves from prosperity. Children instinctively take actions to learn, to explore, to express themselves and to enjoy life. We have been conditioned to ignore those instincts, and we suffer the resulting consequences. This may not be our fault, but it is our responsibility to do something about it. Who else will, if not you?

You do not have to wait another second to allow positive changes to begin. Reading these pages is a beginning. You start by absorbing the ideas. Then imagine what changes you would like to take place in your work or personal life. This is naturally followed by actions based on more prosperous principles. These simple methods have created powerful results for almost every individual who has persistently tried them.

So, continue reading. The time you spend with these ideas is an investment in your journey to more abundance. There is no pressure to take drastic actions. Reading is an action. Discussing ideas is an action. Using your imagination is an action. When you are ready to practice some of these concepts, you will have successfully listened to your instincts and inner messages and have done something to

       Give Yourself a Raise

follow them. The willingness to take actions based on new ideas and principles is the basis for all of the positive outcomes enjoyed by myself, my friends, and my clients.

The time to change is now. Congratulations. By even considering these ideas, as with any new ideas, you have made a great beginning.

MOVING BEYOND YOUR INSECURITY

Our deepest fear is not that we are inadequate. Our deepest fear is that we are powerful beyond measure. It is our light, not our darkness, that most frightens us. We ask ourselves, who am I to be brilliant, gorgeous, talented and fabulous? Actually, who are you not to be? You are a child of God. Your playing small doesn't serve the world. There's nothing enlightened about shrinking so that other people won't feel insecure around you. We were born to make manifest the glory ... that is within us. It's not just in some of us; it's in everyone. And as we let our own light shine, we unconsciously give other people permission to do the same. As we are liberated from our own fear, our presence automatically liberates others.

Nelson Mandela
from 1994 Inaugural Speech

It seems odd that we would be afraid of greater prosperity and abundance. Yet, so many of us are afraid, even terrified, of moving past our familiar, yet unsatisfying circumstances. We experience gnawing insecurity and anxiety at even the thought of change. Many of us are frightened of ourselves -- of being authentic, self-caring, self-led, and highly visible ("shining") in the world. We are taught to be self-deprecating and self-depriving. We learn to seek the approval of others (while denying ourselves) and depend upon their validation that we have acted in "appropriate" ways. This naturally creates anger, self-blame, and insecurity that can plague us and prevent us from moving out boldly into the world.

Approval seeking and insecure interpretations can come to imprison us. We may not know how to take a realistic view of our strengths and our weaknesses. Whether we are very public or private people, we can always hide our real selves and real potential to keep us safe from possible rejection.

Mr. Mandela offers an incredible perspective to us -- brave, magnificent and inspiring beyond expression. Shall we take up the challenge he has so lovingly presented us? Shall we move beyond our fears? Or, shall we say that "shining" and manifesting our "inner glory" is not for us -- only theory and words, a condition that is not obtainable? Your answer can decide the course and quality of your life.

I mentioned earlier that the simple plan I espouse for greater prosperity and abundance entails considering and absorbing new ideas, imagining changes to be made, and then taking new actions based on new concepts. In each phase of change, we will be challenging old beliefs that have kept us feeling inadequate. By facing these false assumptions, we liberate ourselves from the deprivation consciousness that has held us back for so long.

Moving Past Your Conditioning

Before we begin to get into specific ideas and philosophies, it is important to address the issue of how we came to believe, act upon and reinforce self-depriving and self-defeating behaviors.

Whether we are aware of it or not, we all have belief systems. We learned to view and interpret the world, ourselves, and our surroundings through the filter of those beliefs. Accordingly, we operate (take action or refrain from taking action) based upon these deeply ingrained ideas. No one had to stop and teach us these views. We learned them as naturally as we learned the language our parents speak. It is because we assimilated them so naturally they do not seem like a viewpoint. They seem like reality. It is later in our lives, when we face internal conflicts in moving ahead or experience the pains of unsuccessful living, that problems with our perspective come to our attention. We may not be aware, however, that *the problem is with our perspective*. We may falsely believe that our current circumstances or another person's problems stand in the way of our progress.

If you falsely think all of your current beliefs (attitudes) are real, right and justifiable, you will fortify the barrier that keeps you from making positive changes. Therefore, if this book is to be helpful to you, you might assume that there are some self-restricting and self-depriving beliefs that are keeping you from prosperous thinking and abundant living. If your insecurity is stopping you, or if you feel stuck and uncertain (unable to move past your conditioning), then you can assume that some of your attitudes need adjusting. If you wish to enjoy greater success, as it was defined earlier, consider operating under the assumption that it is primarily your self-defeating beliefs that are holding you back.

Once you can accept the basic premise that a shift in attitude is the most powerful force to create change, you have begun to free yourself from your fears. You can learn to move ahead despite all of your negative thoughts, feelings, and viewpoints. They may keep resurfacing, and even intensify, as you try to do things differently. This is natural. For most of us, they will, however, subside as we practice and assimilate new, health-engendering ideas.

SURVIVAL FEAR

As much as each of us possess a survival instinct to keep alive, there is a survival instinct for our personalities as well. That is why it can be frightening and painful to make certain shifts in our lives. No matter how self-defeating some of our thoughts and interpretations are, they have become part of our personality condition and do not want to die easily. If we have enough understanding to try something new, or enough motivation, we can challenge these old beliefs. We can learn to withstand the emotional intensity of changing and make greater self-care and fulfillment a part of our new personality. Then, fears can come and go and no longer rule us.

It is my observation, from much experience, that almost all of us can move beyond our insecurity. We only need to open our minds to the possibility that we can learn, despite obstacles, to speak a new language. It may not be the language of our parents and authority figures, but it is a language with words, ideas and images of internal fortitude, capability, and power.

SURVIVE OR THRIVE?

CHAPTER 4

> *I hate my exercise bike. I keep riding and riding*
> *and it doesn't go anywhere. It's too much like my life.*
> Steve Skrovan, a comedian

We all know what "just surviving" is like. It is struggling just to maintain ourselves in a boring, upsetting or overwhelming situation. We come to feel that if we are not moving ahead we are losing ground. If our situation does not change, we begin to backslide, or at the very least, withstand a great deal of frustration with no end in sight. This will happen in any area of our lives where our needs go unmet. Some of us may attempt to escape into activities and even addictions to distract us from the distress of our circumstances. This only makes matters worse or, at minimum, prolongs the stress of merely surviving.

Ultimately, we need to make choices to find new approaches to our circumstances. Or, by ignoring the facts, we make a choice by default to, as Thoreau said, "lead lives of quiet desperation." I assume you would rather flourish.

What do we need to do to thrive and flourish? We need to change ourselves by changing our beliefs and our behavior. How can we change our beliefs? By understanding that beliefs are just a series of reinforced thoughts and interpretations. Thoughts and interpretations can be ignored, acted upon, or changed. How can we change our behavior? By becoming willing to act upon, new concepts (proposed beliefs) and withstand any feelings, impulses, or negative thoughts that would have us abandon our efforts.

Confronting Our Beliefs

When confronted by alternatives that challenge our current beliefs, we may argue. In many cases, however, we may be quick to agree with another view. Yet, secretly, we still dismiss new ideas and stay with our familiar perspective. New ideas may conflict with the reality we have lived with for so long. In other words, we may be able to intellectually understand and even agree with ideas that could move us ahead, yet still *operate* on the negative belief that a new job, new home, more money, better relationships, etc., are not likely or possible for us.

It is imperative to understand that beliefs are not facts; they are philosophies. That is why they can change -- because philosophies can change. Who among us has not changed their views upon growing older and learning more about ourselves? We grow past some of our old beliefs, yet cling tightly to others that no longer serve us. This creates a conflict of feelings and we can experience a good deal of confusion, doubt, and ambivalence. We want to move ahead as our experience tells us we can, yet we hold back as some of our beliefs tell us not to venture forth.

Most of us have evidence that change has been good for us, but our fears (negative beliefs) may only let us go so far in areas where we feel threatened. That is why we can agree that changes need to occur, yet not do anything about it. We can get into the habit of talking and complaining about how things need to be different, but this is just intellectual dodging while we keep depriving ourselves. Continually talking about what needs to be changed, without operating differently, becomes depriving in and of itself. On the other hand, if we decide to act differently (based upon new thoughts and beliefs), despite feelings of insecurity, we can reap enormous benefits. Your dominant system of beliefs determines your attitudes, your actions, and your abundance or lack thereof. If things are to change for the better, it is here we can effectively begin.

To thrive in our environment and our endeavors, we need to learn to spot the beliefs that keep us struggling and surviving and decide to change them. This is not as difficult as you might imagine. We can literally reverse the habits that we have reinforced over many years in a lot less time we have been living with them. Even if you have not exercised for thirty years, if you begin regular physical activity, you can feel better in a month or two, in six months you will definitely see a marked change in your overall well-being, and in a year you can have a very healthy cardiovascular system. We can change our self-depriving and self-defeating habits in a similar way. Yes, it will take effort and take some time, but it will not take the rest of your life. Furthermore, you will see progress and experience achievements along the way. Since all of us are "set in our ways" to some degree, it will not always be easy. You can learn, however, to flourish regardless of how long you have been struggling until now.

It is never too late to begin improving the quality of your professional and personal life. To raise the level of your prosperity, you will confront beliefs that have long held you back. You can begin to thrive by simply understanding that it is within your ability to do so. You need to know that the human body *and* mind responds remarkably to better habits and healthier practices. It is up to you to use the astonishing recuperative power and adaptability that we all possess. You can make the transition from surviving to thriving, if you are willing to try new methods that can take you there.

GIVE YOURSELF A RAISE
CHAPTER 5

> *Your vision will become clear ... when you*
> *can look into your own heart.*
> Carl Jung

Sometimes you will be the benefactor of a kind universe. A promotion, job opportunity, inheritance, gift or the like will come to you without any effort whatsoever on your part. This can be wonderful indeed. However, it is extremely implausible, if not impossible, that you will be able to live your life abundantly on the basis that the world will always provide for you without your conscious effort to improve your circumstances. There can be a new chapter in your life, but it is you who must write it. In your professional and personal endeavors, it is up to you to conceive goals and accomplish them. You are the author of the changes you wish to make.

Many of us fall prey to the false notion that the world makes life harder for us. Our boss, our landlord, the bank, our neighbors, our co-workers, our relatives, the economy, the government, etc., all do have an effect on us. However, this does not invalidate the fact that, ultimately, we are self-led, self-defined, and self-determined individuals -- even if we do not see ourselves as such.

Almost everything in life is elective. This means we choose to do it. We choose to live where we live, work where we work, eat what we eat, and talk with the people we want to talk with. It may seem like we "have to" work for a living, get married, take care of our kids, pay taxes, keep a roof over our heads, talk to our family and friends, celebrate holidays, play politics at work, or get an education. This does not even begin to mention all the daily tasks most of us address such as fixing meals, paying bills, cleaning house, making phone calls, taking a shower, shopping, opening mail, etc. However, we do not have to do any of these things. The fact is we have elected to do them. There are thousands, if not millions, of others who refuse to do or avoid some of the things we think we *have to* do.

Yet, if we did not do some of these things, we know we would be acting irresponsibly. We agree we need to be somewhat responsible in our lives. After all, we could not get along in the world if we were totally irresponsible. We know we need to do some things to feel even a minimum of self-respect.

How is it, then, that we can be responsible enough to maintain our lives and do a good share of what we believe is "required" of us, yet not seem to feel the same kind of responsibility toward elevating the quality of our lives? The answer is we have been conditioned to adopt a set of standards that have been set for us by others. (If we retaliate against certain standards, we often adopt the standards of the "non-conformist.") Even our view of the improvements we need to make are often based on and can be greatly influenced by the standards of our peers and the society around us. If so influenced, we judge our growth and success by standards others have made; and, therefore, automatically (and often falsely) believe we should strive to live up to those standards as well.

We are interesting creatures. If given requirements, most of us will do what is necessary to meet them. If given the choice as to what we would like to do, we are often confused because we do not know what standard to measure our own desires by. Many of us have a vague or general notion of how things need to be different, but do not know quite what to do or even where to begin. We keep our routines -- too often waiting for something "out there" to change -- desperately wanting relief from the pressure of the responsibilities and standards we believe we "have to" meet. Rarely, if ever, do we stop and recognize that almost everything we are doing is a choice that we have elected to make. We do not realize that what we do on a daily basis is something we can change. To do so, we must truly understand we are, by nature, self-led, self-defined, and self-determined. We would need to see what we are doing as our choice, not a responsibility that has been put upon us.

If we are to enjoy greater abundance in our lives, we need to become willing to discover those things that will make us feel genuinely successful and satisfied. To do this we need to take responsibility for how much money we make, who we associate with, who we work with, and what we do on a daily basis. We need to realize that if we want a raise, it is we who need to create a standard or goal for ourselves, not wait for our clients or boss to give us more money. We must *internally* give ourselves a raise by making a decision that we genuinely want and deserve one. Furthermore, we must see what we want as reasonable to request and obtain. Then we pursue it. This is truly being responsible. In this instance, it is coming to a decision to make more money and persisting in our attempts to get it. In doing so, we show our clear intention. It is the inner strength of our decision, and the gentle persistence of our intentions, that ultimately determine whether we get our raise -- and most other things in life.

Be responsible for the choices you make and see them as such. If you do this, you can raise your income and raise your level of satisfaction. You can raise your ability to discover and pursue what you need and raise your dormant dreams and go after them. You can decide to raise the quality of your personal and professional relationships. If you take responsibility for where you are in you your life, you automatically raise your awareness. As you work to stay awake and aware, you can learn to listen to and follow your instincts. As you continue to accept the fact you are self-led, self-defined, and self-determined, you will practice new ways of operating in the world which will keep your consciousness raised and lead you to abundant living.

MOVING ON FROM PEOPLE

What if someone does not agree with your intention and decision to make a change? For example, if you have given yourself a raise (decided internally to have one), others, obviously, will need to cooperate. However, the specific individuals in your life *today* do not need to cooperate with you. If you decide to raise the quality of your life in any area, you need *some* individuals *at some point in time* to agree with you. However, they need not be in your life at this moment. If your boss will not give you an appropriate raise, and you are going to be truly responsible to yourself, you must look for another boss or company that places a higher value on your services and is willing to give you what you need.

We are faced with accepting a simple premise. We must -- first, last, and always -- take responsibility for raising the quality of our professional and personal lives. It is we who must internally decide to do things differently for ourselves, venture out into the world to follow these goals, and attract others who will support us in thinking more prosperously and living more abundantly. We may grow beyond others in doing so. Yet, we are not so much leaving these people -- but the deprivation they symbolize -- behind.

THE GENTLE APPROACH

Once we have decided to give more abundance to ourselves in some way, how do we go about achieving it? Do we wake up each morning, grit our teeth and move out forcefully into the world "taking no prisoners?" Do we keep going until we succeed or "die trying?" Do we blindly "just do it?" Hardly, and quite the contrary. We pursue our goals and desires with a gracious and generous spirit -- treating ourselves with as much patience and encouragement as we would a child who is learning to walk. We help ourselves by thoughtfully considering and learning new tools and, also, by becoming willing to follow common sense principles that will free us.

We need to proceed and allow ourselves to make mistakes. We need to face difficult circumstances and feelings with gentleness. We need to let ourselves be imperfect and learn from our experiences. We need to praise ourselves for the smallest of victories and share our trials and triumphs with others. We need to try and cooperate with and include others in our endeavors. This is how we raise the quality of our circumstances and the quality of our lives.

Any *genuine* success we might attain cannot be reached by applying ridiculously tough standards or pursuing with a hard-driven, unrelenting, and controlling demeanor. A few of us may attain some achievements this way (most of us will not), but virtually none of us will enjoy any lasting satisfaction from them. Indeed, to raise the level of any area in our lives, we need to make a commitment to doing so. However, we can operate with gentle and patient persistence as we move ahead. Otherwise, we may continue to set ourselves up for failure which weighs upon our spirit. To give yourself a raise means more than mere attainment of financial, professional or personal goals; it also means gently freeing and nurturing your inner spirit. Only in this way can we truly experience a sense of abundant living.

SUCCESS AND SPIRITUALITY

Why do we wish to become more successful? Do you want to enjoy more financial freedom? Do you want to have greater influence and the ability to create change at home, work or in the community? There are negative motivations for wanting success such as wanting to control other human beings, but most of us desire accomplishment for positive reasons. We can view success as giving us the opportunity to do things that are more satisfying. We may also view success as an affirmation of our own value in the world. Others of us want to experience satisfying work or personal relationships as part of our success. When we conjure up a picture of our "successful self," we may see a person who is powerful, happy, and free. As we imagine different scenarios in which we see ourselves, most of us envision images in which we feel satisfaction and a light and contented spirit. There is a universal desire each of us shares to experience these feelings. Our visions and goals may be highly individualized and separate, but the need to find joy and meaning is part of our human psychological nature and underlies our desires. We often get off the track and focus on external success alone rather than bearing in mind our need to have an internal success and contentment.

The root word of spirituality is **spirit**. Therefore, if we view **spirit**uality as the refreshment and continued invigoration of our own human spirit, then whether or not we believe in a Divine Creator, God, Higher Power, or Infinite Universal Intelligence, we can always focus on that wise and gentle part of ourselves that lives "beneath" our daily routines. It is our unique, individual, and undefinable inner spirit that has the capacity to give us guidance, bring us comfort, help us to act with trust, enable us to let go when we want to hold on, help us change and grow, act with courage, and creatively solve problems. Our inner spirit not only has the capacity to send us messages and guidance, it demands that we listen to it. If we deny the inner messages coming to us, we can remain miserable in a situation despite our attempts to change it. In other words, we may frustrate and exhaust ourselves trying to better a futile situation. Yet, we continue to agonize because we are not listening to our inner spirit (wisdom) which is telling us to move on from the situation. Our conscious mind will only continue to suffer if we do not listen to our inner messages. This means our individual spirituality is directly connected to success. We cannot truly attain overall satisfaction and contentment of spirit if we ignore that we possess an inner life as well as an outer life. It is our inner life that holds our beliefs, guides our actions, and truly dominates our outer life. Even if a person defines their inner life as purely emotional, it still holds true that we need to address our emotions (as our overall spirit) and strive to keep them healthy and balanced if we are to live more abundantly.

To give yourself a raise, you will probably need to focus on what truly nourishes and supports your inner life as well as your outer life. You might attain some external success, but if you ignore you are, in part, spiritual *by nature*, you may find yourself unhappy and confused once the initial feelings of accomplishment wear off. Remember, there can be no lasting or true success without the experience of satisfaction and contentment of spirit. There can be satisfaction and contentment only if we listen to what our individual spirit is telling us.

Spirituality does not need to be aligned with religion, mysticism, prayer, or meditation -- though the practice of these has brought much comfort and courage and has created positive change for millions of people. Spirituality needs only to be aligned with success as it relates to your attempts to listen to your inner messages (not negative voices) and act upon them. You can safely trust your genuine instincts -- this is spirituality. You can follow a new direction even though it does not make sense with the way you have been living or what you have been doing -- this is spirituality. You can talk to yourself in a kind and encouraging manner -- this is spirituality. You can ask the wisest part of yourself for answers to important questions and let go until the answers appear -- this is spirituality. You can talk to someone to help you gain a perspective that will calm you, comfort you, and give you hope -- this is spirituality. Practicing spirituality is an essential element in genuine success. It is the refreshment and invigoration of your spirit which is vital to your well being.

Whatever you believe about this subject, or however you frame or define the idea of your own spirituality, make sure to view your goals and desires in line with nourishing your inner life. This means developing a willingness to follow your inner guidance, even if you are unsure how to do so. To ignore it means continued and unnecessary stress. In listening to your inner guidance, you raise the quality of your goals and live more abundantly by aiming for both outer achievement and internal satisfaction.

Are You Ready for The Next Step?

To raise the level of your prosperity, you will need to ready yourself by being willing to alter how you think and what you do. Even the slightest shifts in your beliefs and actions can produce tremendous results. The next step, then, involves your willingness to seriously consider some new ideas that may help you. Like most of us, it is likely you operate based on some attitudes that simply hold you back or create self-sabotage. Therefore, a positive shift begins with a willingness on your part to admit that you act upon some deeply ingrained ideas that are self-depriving or self-defeating.

That is why the first and overriding principle (and title of the next chapter) is:

Adopt New Attitudes as Your Basis for Abundant Living.

The willingness to adopt new attitudes does not mean that you instantly accept everything on an internal level. It means that you see the sense in the philosophy and become willing to take reasonable actions based upon it.

For the moment, however, the only thing suggested is to read on. The next step is for you to explore how these principles may apply to you. Think about your situation and how you might use what you find in these pages to improve your circumstances. There is nothing to do but keep an open mind. This is the beginning of awakening your consciousness and allowing yourself to be inspired. As Carl Jung suggested, "your vision will become clear ... when you can look into your own heart."

To give yourself a raise, in every sense of the word, ultimately you must seek, find, and continue to nurture the inspiration to do things differently. You do this by allowing the qualities of growth, courage, and enthusiasm *that are already within you* to be expressed in new, more effective ways.

SECTION II
PRINCIPLES AND
PERSONAL STORIES

This section will examine concepts and ideas that have produced consistent results for individuals who have used them to reach professional and personal goals.

At the end of each chapter, you will find personal stories of my clients' experiences. Each client adopted one or more of the ideas elaborated upon in this section. To maintain their anonymity and privacy, clients' names and certain background facts have been altered. The circumstances of their before-and-after tales and the results of their progress, however, are true. These stories are offered as testimony of theories and principles that, if followed, provide a realistic and genuine opportunity for growth.

Credit for the progress and accomplishment illustrated in each story belongs with the client. I have been their guide and partner in helping them live more abundantly, but they are the ones who have courageously practiced and applied the suggestions and enjoyed the benefits.

Finally, following each story are reminders of the pertinent principles that were discussed. These reminders are encapsulated in short statements, declarations, and axioms, if you will. They are presented in the event you want to refer briefly to the main ideas in a particular chapter. Some individuals may wish to write out particular reminders and put them in a place where they can be easily seen.

Those of you who find affirmations helpful, may even wish to substitute the word "I" for the word "you" for those reminder statements that inspire you. Reading and repeating sound ideas or inspirational thoughts to yourself can stimulate and re-train your thinking. They can help you address an important decision more effectively, calm you in a stressful situation, or even give you a more positive or optimistic outlook in conducting your day. Read them at the beginning or end of your day, or anytime you feel the need for additional support.

ADOPT NEW ATTITUDES AS YOUR BASIS FOR ABUNDANT LIVING

CHAPTER 6

> *What we teach ourselves with our thoughts and attitudes is up to us.*
> Anonymous

In Section I, you have seen many words used interchangeably: beliefs, principles, philosophies, attitudes, and perspectives. For the purposes of this discussion, they all amount to the same thing: the dominant thoughts from which you conduct your life.

If we are to improve our circumstances and live more abundantly, we need to challenge and alter our thoughts, interpretations, and judgments -- shift our attitudes where they are detrimental to us. Most of us do not have totally self-defeating attitudes. We can observe, interpret, judge, and react positively to many events in our lives. The degree to which we interpret and judge ourselves and situations poorly is the degree to which we need to shift our attitudes.

One example might be asking for more money for the work we perform. We may think we deserve more money, but our overall view of the situation (interpretations and judgments) may interfere with our goal. A host of self-defeating thoughts, which form an attitude, can keep us from asking for more money or leaving for a better paying job.

All of us could come up with numerous examples of how someone's thinking keeps them in frustration and distress. If we know something about them and their prior conditioning, we may find it understandable that they act upon negative thinking and behavior no matter how much it hurts them. It is common wisdom that we tend to repeat what we know. Like all of us at times, they may not interpret and judge their circumstances in light of their own best interests. It is probable they have adopted the attitudes and assessments of others who did not know how to be self-caring.

In stating that you need to adopt new attitudes to raise your level of prosperity, this book will be asking you to shift your thinking. This only requires that you become willing to consider different beliefs and contemplate acting upon them. Most of us will experience old doubts and negative assessments as we decide to adopt a new way of interpreting, judging, and acting. This is completely normal and expected. What is important is to stay with a new attitude persistently until it has a good chance to work. In doing this, we can eventually transform self-defeating thoughts into thoughts that lead to positive, self-fulfilling prophesies.

Whether you simply want to make a few adjustments or are in severe crisis, the route is the same. We need to consider adjusting our thinking and *then* make plans to take ourselves to a better place.

A Different Question

Have you ever asked yourself these questions: What would I need to think and believe to improve my present situation? What attitudes can I take that would be helpful in my situation?

If you have questioned yourself in this manner, you are very rare indeed. In former days, I certainly never asked myself these questions. I was too busy scrambling and surviving to look at my attitudes. Each day's crisis begged me to DO something. Since I was always doing something or not doing something based on my old, self-defeating beliefs, nothing changed for the better -- only for the worse.

As you continue through the following chapters, begin to ask yourself what attitudes you would like to believe and act upon.

You may question some of what is being presented here. Yet, it is strongly suggested to you that you fully examine these ideas and thoroughly consider them. We can get into the habit of too easily dismissing things that might help us. How many of our problems result from us dismissing ourselves? We dismiss our wants and needs. We dismiss our natural talents. We dismiss our capabilities. We dismiss obstacles as too hard or too time-consuming to overcome. We dismiss our ability to influence others. We dismiss the possibility that others can help us. We dismiss the idea that we should change, and we think, if others would do things differently, we would have all the opportunity and happiness we needed. Begin to look at how you may be dismissing yourself and, as you read, keep an open mind to whatever you find unusual or seemingly too difficult to follow.

Again, for the moment, do not DO anything. Just begin to question your attitudes. What attitudes would you like to take toward the circumstances you want to improve? The principles that follow are meant to offer you some possibilities and inspire some answers.

THE NUTS AND BOLTS

The primary reason for writing this book was to the share the successes of individuals who made exciting progress in their professional and personal endeavors. No book could encompass the entirety of their stories and all the principles and ideas they practiced. However, the results and improvements experienced by a wide variety of people were significant enough to discuss some of these important ideas and make them available for the consideration of others. If you are skeptical, good! Because only experience and patient practice at acting upon more prosperous beliefs will give you the *internal knowledge* that these ideas and principles work. In other words, you are not being asked to take these ideas on faith. When you are ready, try them.

The remaining primary subjects being presented in this section are:

Welcome the Natural Order of Change
Prepare Yourself to Act on Better Opportunities
Get Clear and Communicate Clearly
Simplify Your Choices
Stay in Current Reality
Make What You Want Important
Follow Abundance
Act on the Assumption That Success Is Possible
View Setbacks as Assets
Apply Perseverance
Allow Yourself to Be Prosperous

The above concepts are discussed for your consideration. They are not commandments or immutable laws. They amount to making a shift in your perspective. If we change our perspective, we can change the circumstances and experiences of our professional and personal lives.

—✦✦— HE BECAME WILLING TO CHANGE —✦✦—

A man had just broken up with his live-in girlfriend. She ended the relationship and asked him to move out of their one bedroom apartment in Manhattan. His financial circumstances added to his stress. A modest unemployment check every two weeks barely sustained him, but there was no money to move, to pay for rent, or to make any purchases beyond food and basic expenses. There were no savings and his relatives could not lend him money. Bad credit made bank loans or credit card use out of the question.

Roz, a compassionate friend, let him stay in her large one-room apartment. He slept on a foam mattress on the floor. He would lay awake at night anxiously thinking about his situation. He knew the emotional and financial dependence upon his girlfriend was the final play in a losing game. He had managed to live dependently on others for many years. By this point, time had run out on his self-destructive behavior. He had numerous creditors and was overwhelmed with bills, unpaid taxes, and personal debt. Opening the mailbox terrified him. He accumulated a huge pile of unopened mail. If the mail remained unopened, he was safe, or so he thought, from problems he could not face.

With great resistance, he began to look for work. After two months of searching, the results were dismal and depressing. He knew he could not stay with Roz indefinitely, yet time was ticking away. Necessity being the mother of invention, he came up with an idea to make money. Good at organizing events, he decided to hold a conference and charge people to attend. If successful, this would give him enough money to move and hopefully buy time for a little while longer.

Through hard work and luck, the conference was a modest financial success. The moment the conference was over, however, Roz asked when he was moving. She became, in a sense, another creditor, wanting to know when he was going to take care of the problem.

Now, he lived with a "creditor." He still had no stable means of income.

His problems with creditors, bills and taxes were overwhelming. So, two days after Roz asked when he was leaving, he finally decided to get help with these issues. Intense pain and fear finally made him ready for something -- anything. His distress broke his denial. He simply and finally became a person willing to change.

—◇◇◇—

After a time, he uncovered a primary problem. He had been underpaid and had not been earning enough money for almost all of his life. Contrary to what he had believed, spending recklessly was not the real issue. There was a strong belief that he would always lack money. This created most of his struggles. Expenses were met by getting into more and more debt. Things others considered essentials, like going to the dentist or doctor, buying quality clothes, and taking vacations were luxuries and unaffordable to him. "Those things are for others, not me," he had always thought. Yet, despite this conditioning, he became willing to adopt new attitudes and act on different principles. He became teachable and began to make progress.

Since there were new attitudes, there were new actions being carried out. He opened all of those stockpiled envelopes. (Ironically, two of the unopened envelopes contained checks to him.) Even if he did not know what to do with the contents, he opened his mailbox and every letter, every day. Actions were taken to find work and money started coming in. Communication with creditors began and small regular debt repayments followed. He consistently asked for and received help from others with more experience. He adopted and tried their approaches and successfully adapted them to his situation. There was a remarkable transformation happening.

He was astonished at how willingness to adopt new attitudes and act on different beliefs and principles created changes in him. As he learned to give to himself and face his fears, he found himself in a better living space with a better income. He learned to save money as well as pay his debts. (At the time of the writing of this book, he has settled 41 out of 44 debts that were incurred over 14 years, without declaring bankruptcy. The remaining debts are in the process of being settled.)

After much success in these new approaches, he began to share what he learned with others. In time, he conducted workshops and attracted private clients to help them with their businesses, careers, finances, and personal goals. His difficulties in the past became a valuable asset to others who were seeking to improve their situations or elevate themselves to greater prosperity.

In becoming willing to adopt new attitudes and act upon new principles, an amazing financial reversal occurred. There is now a thriving business, with successful clients. Even more importantly, where there was deprivation, confusion, and destructive behavior there is prosperous living, direction, self-care, and gratitude. Where there was self-denial and fear there is much greater self-acceptance, satisfaction, faith, and freedom of spirit.

By now, you may have guessed, the story is mine.

The Author

REMINDERS:

- You can adopt new attitudes and beliefs to elevate the circumstances and experiences of your life.

- You can explore new ideas with an open mind.

- You can act upon a principle, without fully believing it, to demonstrate your willingness to do things differently.

- You can transform negative thoughts into thoughts that lead to positive, self-fulfilling prophesies.

WELCOME THE NATURAL ORDER OF CHANGE

CHAPTER 7

*The two things I fear most are that
things will stay exactly the way they are and things will change.*
Brad Lempert

The idea that we need to change is not a problem; our resistance to and fear of change creates the problems. It is one of life's curiosities that something so fundamentally sound is so difficult to accept. Many of us become very frightened by change and yet hate routine. The spark of adventure and exploration we all possess seems to give way to clinging to familiarity at all costs. There is an Italian saying that captures the essence of how so many of us operate. It roughly translates to: "Better the devil you know, than the devil you don't." That is fine if you do not mind living with the devil.

Change is part of life. It will happen in a natural order with or without our acceptance of it. We can try to avoid change, yet it will not let us escape the consequences of doing so. Usually, change does not create chaos -- but fighting change does.

The reason we dislike the idea of change is because of what it means to us. If we identify change with fear, loss, or failure, then we are apt to avoid it at all costs. However, if we learn to view change as natural, normal, and healthy, we can learn to embrace it, going through any discomfort it may bring and finding ourselves reinvigorated in our new circumstances.

For most of us, we learned our reactions to change at a very early age. If we had guardians who let us explore and grow in a safe environment, we came to view change as interesting, pleasurable and even exciting. If we were lucky enough to explore safely, we do not see change as a threat to our existence or well-being. Conversely, if we were too restricted, we came to fear change as unknown and possibly hazardous. We learned that change is dangerous. If we were neglected as children, we had to depend upon our own resources far too much and far too early in life. If so, we were without enough guidance and protection, and we were too little and too vulnerable to deal with the overwhelming and giant world in which we lived. We learned that we were inadequate to deal with new and startling events alone and came to experience change as distressing, requiring enormous effort, and emotionally damaging.

It is truly unfortunate that so many of us have come to identify change with **Danger**. No wonder we resist change! Who would consciously put themselves in a dangerous situation? In order, to embrace change as a natural part of our lives, we need to remove the idea of Danger we have come to associate with it. As we tried to explore, learn, and naturally express our needs as children, there may have been genuine threats in the form of abandonment, withdrawal, punishment, rejection, or neglect from our guardians and authority figures. To a child, these are actual dangers. To adults, they are not. Over the course of our adult lifetime, there are very *very* *very* few (was 'very' said enough times?), if any, genuine threats to our existence or personalities through the process of change. In almost every instance, the sense of Danger is a leftover and can be safely ignored. We need, then, to ignore the false projections of Danger and listen to the messages beckoning us to move ahead.

EVOLUTION, NOT REVOLUTION

No matter what our current circumstances, they will change in some way. For the most part, they will do this in an evolutionary way. Upon growing more mature, there will be natural shifts in our professional pursuits, our relationships, our bodies, etc. If we can embrace this idea, we will not be caught off guard when our environment or our needs shift. Where we may now be single and carefree, over time we discover a wish to start a home and family. Where we may now be content to earn more money, we begin to yearn for more satisfying work. Where we may now be single-minded about individual pursuits, we begin to seek group and community activities.

No matter who we are, we will change. Each of our lives has an evolution. This evolution points us toward our human need to grow. It may involve others, it may not. But, internal yearnings to do things differently will call to us. If we do not pay attention to these inner messages, we suffer the consequences of ignoring them. Our inner or outer environment shifts and beckons us to come along. The comfort or contentment we once experienced can turn to frustration. Through frustration, we find we are outgrowing situations that were once acceptable to us. These growing pains are natural and desirable. Without them, we might never do anything to take a proactive lead in our lives.

All we need to do is listen, explore, and gently follow our inner messages. We do not need to revolt and make drastic efforts. When we revolt by either ignoring the internal and external messages, or by going at top speed to "get it over with," we can create obstacles that put us further back than where we started. If we are afraid of the water but would like to enjoy it, we do not need to walk thirty feet away to avoid the pool *or* dive into the deep end. If we would truly like to take a cool dip, if the water looks refreshing yet frightening, all we need to do is stand at the shallow end and contemplate wading in. We do not have to go in -- only contemplate wading in.

We can apply the process of evolutionary change to most of our goals. Let's carry the analogy of the pool further. Let us say that a grown man had become terrified of water and feared drowning in it. As a child, he could swim and enthusiastically enjoyed the public pool. Somewhere through the years certain fears crept up in him that made him associate being in the water with danger -- believing he may not be able to save himself from disaster if he were to swim again. Let us further assume that he strongly wants to enjoy water. In the hot summer, the pool in his apartment complex almost seems to invite him in. His dilemma is that he would really like to go in the water, yet he does not want to go in if he cannot enjoy it fully. Staying in the shallow end would be quite unrewarding and embarrassing for him. Here is a process he could follow to attain his goal.

First, he would have to assume that in an evolutionary process no effort is too small. Each action of the mind or body would be a simple step in the change he is being called to make. I would suggest that he repeat each step as many times, for as many days, as necessary before moving onto the next one.

Step 1: Go to the edge of the shallow end of the pool. Look at the water and just think about going in. Imagine how refreshing the water could be, if you did not have fear about being in it.

Step 2: Sit at the shallow end and hang your feet into the water for a few minutes.

Step 3: Put on swimwear and just wade in to water no more than 3 feet deep. Crouch or sit in the water up to your neck.

Step 4: Move around in the 3-foot depth and do a few gentle arm strokes to and from each side of the pool. Do this for a few minutes up to a half an hour.

Step 5: Get in the shallow water. Do a few laps side to side in the shallow end. When you are done with that, try holding your breath once and put your head under water for a second or two.

Step 6: Continue side to side laps in shallow water. Also, slowly increase the time you are holding your breath under water until you can do so to a count of 10 (or, if you desire, challenge yourself gently up to 20 seconds).

Step 7: Wade out to 4- or 5-foot depth, making sure your head and shoulders are above water and your feet can easily touch the bottom of the pool. Remember, you have practiced your strokes and can hold your breath for 10 seconds or more. So, if you get scared, you can always swim back to more shallow water.

Step 8: Keep practicing your strokes and breathing in "safe" water. A little at a time let yourself slowly inch out toward deeper water. You should now have the arm strength to dog paddle and keep yourself afloat, if for only a short while. Stay next to the side of the pool, so that you can grab the edge if you get anxious.

Step 9: Coax yourself to dog paddle off the side of pool in water that comes up to your nose and mouth. Let your head go beneath the water a few times and grab the side of the pool when you have succeeded.

Step 10: Little by little venture out toward the center of the pool, swimming back to the side when you feel your anxiety rising.

Step 11: Return to shallow water and do one or more laps, one at a time, <u>under water</u> from side to side. Increase, little by little, the depth at which you do your under water side to side laps.

Step 12: Stop at the center during one of your under water laps, dog paddle for a short time and continue to swim *under* water to the other side.

Step 13: In "safe" water, submerge and touch the bottom of the pool. Coaxing yourself gently into deeper water, day by day, until you are in the pool's maximum depth. When you come up, dog paddle and slowly swim to one side.

Step 14: You are now enjoying the full length of the pool. Remember to try new things only until they take you to the "edge of anxiety." When you feel that edge on any given day or with any step, pull back and go to a safe place for yourself. You will marvel at how far you will come in such a short time.

Each small step is part of the larger goal. Evolution happens in this same way. Each small action of mind or body creates the safe foundation to move to the next step. If we push too hard, our anxieties can cause us to blunder or get stuck. If we do not take actions at all, we remain feeling helpless and frustrated.

It is difficult to practice the idea of patient, evolutionary change. In the example above, it would take many small, persistent, repeated steps to achieve the desired result. Yet, years of avoidance and fear can be overcome in a relatively short amount of time. In this example it might take only three or four weeks to reverse a decade of fear. It is possible to do. I know. The example I gave was my own personal experience of learning to enjoy water again.

GO FOR SMALL VICTORIES

The same process applies in making a career shift, expanding a business or working toward any number of goals. You can learn to recognize and listen to the messages and clues that are telling you to move ahead or change your circumstances. You then contemplate the change and take small, persistent actions to move ahead. You do not need to rush as rushing sets off alarms of danger. Focus on small victories. They lay the foundation of change. You can experience extraordinary results from operating a step at a time. You might consider actually praising and endorsing yourself for each step taken, no matter how small, along the way.

Most of us cannot assimilate lasting improvement quickly. We do not want to force ourselves to abruptly change. This means we will integrate and maintain natural changes over time, with repetition fortifying new actions and behavior. At another time, we may be beckoned to grow again.

We may have kept ourselves from moving ahead by trying too hard or not at all. We need only cooperate with and welcome the natural order of change -- doing our best to dispel the myth that there are threats and dangers in moving ahead. Change is best through evolution, not revolution. Small victories can turn into sweet success. Understanding this provides the vehicle by which we can overcome years of negative conditioning.

A NEW ROAD AWAITED HIM
HE NEEDED TO LEARN IT WAS SAFE TO TRAVEL IT

A 32-year-old accountant by the name of Stanley had been working at his father's small company in Brooklyn for many years. Stanley developed a base of his own clients, but primarily served the hundreds of clients his father had developed over 30 years in the business. The job responsibilities were manageable, but he was not very interested in the services he was performing (filing of taxes, reviewing financial records, audits, etc.) Stanley's father, who was 62, hinted he was retiring at some point in the future. Stanley, however, was unexcited at the idea of taking over his father's business. He knew he could earn a living doing so, but he wanted to move forward in his life. Guilt and fearful anticipation of his father's reaction were also a factor. He did not wish to be seen as betraying his father; he only wanted something different for himself. Getting stuck in just earning a paycheck to please others was a trap Stanley did not want to fall into.

—◇◇◇—

It was apparent to me from the beginning that Stanley was experiencing a natural order of change -- growing away from his father's goals toward his own independent needs. He agreed with my assessment of the situation, and we continued to work together and established a regular schedule of consultations. Before taking any action, we examined the concept of the natural order of change during several work sessions. It was evident that internal feelings were beckoning Stanley to grow beyond his father's business. I suggested, if he ignored these internal clues he would continue to feel distressed in his present position. In moving on, I assured him, he was not dishonoring his father's desires; he was honoring his own. Of course, it is natural and inevitable that children continue to grow and, literally and symbolically, leave home.

Stanley came to accept that change was healthy and right -- not a betrayal of any kind. At that point, we discussed the services Stanley would like to provide his own clients. We moved toward the idea of developing a clientele for a new service -- Personal Financial Management.

Developing his own business interests, as his father had done 30 years before, was vital to Stanley's prosperity. Letting go of the family business was a challenging concept for Stanley and it took several months to integrate this idea into his attitude. Only contemplating at first, he began to imagine himself serving individuals in Personal Financial Management. After spending time in this contemplation stage, Stanley began slowly taking actions to open up this possibility, among which included taking classes to increase his knowledge in the area.

A few months later, as fortune would have it, one of his father's clients needed an opinion on investments and money management. His father knew of Stanley's interest in this area and referred the client to his son. His willingness to accept that a natural change was occurring made him ready. When the time came to assess the client's general financial circumstances, Stanley successfully negotiated a financial transaction for the client and made a handsome commission in the process. The philosophy and his vision had become reality. He came to accept he needed to change and grow beyond his familiar situation and proceeded slowly to do so.

During the next year, while still working for his father, Stanley doubled his income providing new services to his own clients. He continues to develop his own clientele and has future plans to rent his own office. Both he and his father are thriving in their separate business ventures. Though the accounting clients provide a resource for his Personal Financial Management services, Stanley is truly moving toward professional independence and enjoying greater satisfaction and income from his work. During the current calendar year, Stanley has a goal to triple the income he had when we began our work together. This would take him into a six figure income, and he is currently right on track to make that sum. He is moving in a non-rushed, step-by-step manner, following clues and his instincts along the way. Stanley's father learned to accept the change that has occurred, and Stanley is learning to welcome change in his professional and personal life.

REMINDERS:

- **Change is healthy, inevitable, and natural. You can welcome it.**

- **There is no danger in growing.**

- **You can allow yourself to change gently and naturally.**

- **It is safe for you to follow the clues that are trying to lead you to a higher level of satisfaction.**

- **You can face and overcome your fears by taking small steps.**

- **Go for small victories.**

Give Yourself a Raise

PREPARE YOURSELF TO ACT ON BETTER OPPORTUNITIES

CHAPTER 8

If you believe you have options, you do.
If you believe you don't, you don't.
Richard Holt

To ready ourselves to take actions that will move us ahead or raise us out of a negative environment, we begin by assuming better opportunities exist. Of course, with negative television and newspaper accounts of the economy, job market, and upsetting social trends, it is difficult to keep an open mind. Also adding to our fears are personal stories of our friends' financial and personal troubles. We can easily buy into the idea that we should stay where we are because "look how bad it is out there." The facts we hear seem to tell us so. If we are out of work we can view the job market as extremely competitive and unfriendly. If we are trying to better our personal lives, we can view society as "going to hell" and see obstacles as insurmountable. "Look at all the evidence, for heaven's sake." The first order of business, then, is to prepare ourselves by becoming willing to act upon the view that there is almost assuredly room for us in the marketplace and there are alternatives in improving our personal lives. Even if we do not know how our goals can be met or where we will end up, we start by assuming our reasonable desires can be attained and better opportunities *are* out there.

The problem with depending upon reports coming from others in our professional or personal endeavors is that we fall prey to conducting ourselves as though we are statistics. The trap of pointing to statistics is that they only demonstrate general trends. If we were to look at nationwide unemployment rates for the past two years, they might go up. However, all of the same individuals did not stay unemployed for the entire two years. We can reasonably assume many of them found jobs, some of whom found better jobs. They were replaced *statistically* by others who lost their jobs. On the personal side, it is statistically true that most women over the age of 35 will not get married. Does this mean that everyone should give up and join the ranks of those who operate their lives according to general trends? Let us hope not.

Personal stories of friends or co-workers who have suffered professional or personal loss or who are "forced" to settle for undesirable situations also promote faulty thinking. The circumstances, capabilities, and, most importantly, attitudes of others do not have to be yours. Therefore, if you decide it so, your opportunities and options will be different from those who live under the tyranny of a general negative view. We all know some individuals who are living examples of exceptions to a variety of professional and social statistics. We can all point to a number of instances in which people who possess the same basic skills have much different incomes, benefits, work environments, and personal lives. By comparison, we can see individuals who are not doing as well do not wish trying to improve their situation and are staying safe. They hold on to "stability," and that is their right. However, from our vantage point we can see that it is possible (and extremely likely) they could tap into their potential, take more action, raise the quality of their lives, and have stability under better conditions, if they allowed themselves, to do so. Many of us could include ourselves among those people. We are staying safe, rather than taking risks to grow and live more prosperously. If this is so, we need to see ourselves as we see them -- having great potential if we can challenge the false notion that the environment primarily dictates our opportunities and success.

The primary problem with daring to conduct ourselves independent of commonly held beliefs and opinions is that it threatens our sense of belonging and opens us up to criticism or ridicule. It is often far easier to commiserate than to draw attention to ourselves by declaring our intention to do well despite what the "party line" has to say. We may face another obstacle in leaving behind negative situations because we get used to them. The discomfort we feel is all too familiar and can keep us hanging on yet unhappy. We can also suffer as we hang on to relationships with people (i.e., bosses, clients, secretaries, colleagues, friends, lovers) that are negative and even abusive. We may *think* we need their help. Or we may *think* we must work with them for the sake of our income. Or we *think* we need a specific person for emotional security. So believing, we postpone attempts to leave negative situations and establish healthier relationships. Too many of us have probably, at some point, stayed in situations or relationships that left us feeling deprived or ill-used for a very long time. In some way, we feel comfortable, even if the overall situation is depressing or pressure-packed. This false feeling of "comfort" can immobilize our natural desire to improve our circumstances. All of us have an attraction to what is familiar.

Operating outside of general opinions and supposed facts takes fortitude. Letting go of familiar yet unsatisfying situations and people takes courage. It means we will be different and unique in attempting to treat ourselves better. We may also outgrow others who seem settled in a negative environment or are unable to move ahead. What we may really be afraid of is leaving others behind. We want to be more satisfied but we may feel guilty, ambivalent and frightened in trying to do so.

We prepare to act upon better opportunities by allowing ourselves to think about leaving our present circumstances or letting go of negative individuals. Leaving situations or ending relationships creates a sense of loss. Most of us do not take loss well, even if what we are losing is holding us down.

It would also be a risk. Facing the unknown is something we may have learned to fear intensely because we think there is a possibility that (a) things will not be any better; or (b) things will be better, but we will not know how to handle more success or responsibility. These fears can create formidable reasons for us to stay in our current situations or relationships. To overcome these fears, we can continue to remind ourselves of a simple truth: we can face challenges, and even adversity, and succeed. Decide, act, face the discomfort and prevail. This is a formula we all have used successfully at some point in our lives. Even in your present circumstances you started anew, learned, adapted, and have grown. It is our innate human adaptability that insures we will adjust to different people, places and circumstances. It is we who need to insist of ourselves that we use these powerful human qualities to put ourselves in better situations or with better people.

THE COMPETITIVE MARKET IS A MYTH

For any one individual, the Competitive Market is not a series of facts. The Competitive Market is a myth based on a belief that if you try to change your circumstances you will be met with insurmountable odds, fail in your attempts, or face ridicule or rejection for taking risks. It may be difficult to understand why you seem to want change when others seem able to tolerate or accept the same situation or people that make you unhappy. Others may actually be satisfied or tolerant of issues you find constantly upsetting. They may also just be in denial or buying into the belief of negative general trends "out there." Holding on to the idea that your experience should be the same as others is a self-defeating thought process. You can challenge the impulse to compare yourself. Again, general trends may be *generally true*. They do not have to be *specifically true* for you.

Each and every client who has come to me unemployed or looking for a better job, and has stayed with the process, has found a position better than the last one they had in their field. This is not a fluke. It came by confronting and dispelling the myths that they could not do better in the marketplace. Despite obstacles and apprehension, they learned to move ahead on the positive principle that better opportunities existed for them.

If you look to what others believe and accept it as your yardstick, you can remain trapped in your thinking and stay compliant, stagnant, and miserable.

DECIDE YOU WILL NOT BE A STATISTIC

We may have fallen into believing that the only options we have are the most obvious ones, which we may see as very limited. In this way, we trap ourselves in fear and immobilize our natural resourcefulness. To see more options, we first assume they exist, even if we cannot yet see them. All of us have evidence in our lives of opportunities popping up at just the right time. We can become ready to capitalize on better opportunities, if we decide they exist.

We begin by challenging ourselves. In the light of your own circumstances, decide that you are willing to treat yourself well by allowing yourself to be in a good situation with good people. Decide to treat the negative assessments of others as their opinions, not facts. You can become willing to change and, therefore, withstand feelings of anxiety and uncertainty rather than seek the comfort of a familiar setting. Decide, then, that you will not act as though you are a statistic.

It is not suggested that you take any action, or that you leave your present job, or let go of negative people, abruptly. Leaving behind negative situations is transitional. It is a process. You begin it by consciously deciding that options exist for you. You do not have to know what other options exist or take immediate action. Yet there is so much more out there for you, if you can slowly strengthen yourself internally to step toward it.

Work on your beliefs. Stop watching negative news accounts of the economy, money-related and social issues. This is not about living in denial. It is refraining from reinforcing the negative and unrealistic idea that you cannot thrive in the world. Avoid the trap of talking with friends about "how bad it is out there." If you run into prospective employers, clients, or average citizens with negative views of the market and opportunities, tell yourself, "This is their reality. It does not have to be mine. There are opportunities for me, even if I cannot see them today." Encourage yourself to move past the fears of others in this way.

Focus on your hopes and your ability to adapt. We have all learned to adapt to depriving experiences. We can also learn to adapt to positive experiences if we decide to treat ourselves as individuals, not statistics, who have the ability to withstand the discomfort of moving ahead.

You have options. It is important that you know this. Your attitudes ultimately determine your opportunities, not the marketplace.

—❧— SHE WAS TIRED OF DOING —❧— TOO MUCH FOR TOO LITTLE

Jane, 40, a textile designer, toiled for a small design firm in Chicago that specialized in fabrics for furniture. With the high cost of city living, her lower-than-average salary barely sustained her. Her debts were high and repaying them kept her feeling quite poor. The owners of the design firm were brothers who came from a wealthy family. All the same, this did not stop them from being penny pinchers and afraid to invest adequately in their business. Influenced by the owners' fearful and controlling attitudes, Jane took on many extra administrative duties because the owners would not hire anyone to do them. She spent just as much time on administration/ marketing (which she truly disliked) as she did on design work (which she loved). When she spoke to colleagues and friends about leaving her job, Jane kept hearing how competitive and tight the market was, and that salaries were down. This frightened her. She did not feel she could be without a job. Trying a few side jobs bring in some extra money, Jane could not devote enough time to any of them to see much income. At work, the two brothers often disagreed, and Jane's ideas and suggestions were routinely rejected. Constantly "crying poor," the owners refused to pay better salaries or issue long overdue raises. Jane spent four years being underpaid, unappreciated, and unhappy, and she wanted something better. Her "stable" job was keeping her economically, emotionally, and physically drained. She wanted to move on, but was unclear and anxious about how to do so.

———◇◇◇———

I met Jane when she was visiting a client of mine in New York and she came in for an initial consultation. This first meeting went very well and we agreed to continue working by conducting consultations via long-distance telephone. The first task at hand was to find out what Jane wanted for herself in terms of income, job responsibilities, and work environment. At first, she kept telling me how difficult it would be to get a position that really met these needs. I did not argue. I just kept asking her to take an objective view of her talents and capabilities and asked if there were companies that might be able to use someone like her -- not her, of course, but someone like her.

After many discussions, Jane made the internal decision she needed to work elsewhere. She became prepared not to let the common belief in a tight market stop her efforts. This was a significant and courageous internal action. As she began to explore other possibilities, we worked on her attitudes and beliefs about the marketplace and endeavored to avoid the trap of taking on a general trend as her specific reality. This challenged the myths so many people fall prey too.

She stopped trying to make money from side jobs, which were not fruitful, and concentrated on moving forward to a better job. Though anxious about what she would find, Jane used her creativity and resourcefulness to begin making contacts through friends and professional acquaintances. These contacts had always been available to her, but Jane had not yet been mentally prepared to use them. The process of becoming ready to leave her job took several months, but it paid off. Through these efforts, an exciting position was eventually offered.

In her new firm, she now supervises a staff of four in the design department. Jane does not have to do marketing or be in charge of general office administration. Others are hired to do that. Previously bypassed ideas and suggestions are being met with appreciation and respect. After only a few months, Jane's contributions became vital to her new company. Her new salary for the first year, the icing on the cake, was 35% higher than that of her previous job.

Isn't it amazing that, after years of being afraid to move, something better came along when Jane prepared herself to act on new opportunities, made the internal decision to change jobs, and became willing to risk leaving behind her familiar yet frustrating setting?

REMINDERS:

- There are more options and opportunities for you than you can currently see.

- You have the ability to adapt and adjust to new situations.

- You can internally strengthen yourself to look for better circumstances before taking action.

- Statistics are general. Act as an individual and your individual experience will be positive.

- You do not have to listen to or expose yourself to negative accounts of those who may be struggling.

- Your attitudes and actions will be different than those of others and so will your results.

GET CLEAR AND COMMUNICATE CLEARLY

CHAPTER 9

> *I don't know what I want, but I know I don't have it.*
> Anonymous

There is great power in being clear. Clarity can calm us, motivate us, and give us great influence with others. It presents us to the world as capable and confident, which is always very magnetic. First, we need to get clear with ourselves, and then others.

Many obstacles can stand in our way of getting clear and communicating clearly. Primary among these obstacles are the fear of defining ourselves and the need for approval. In being clear, we may fear we will lose something we already have or fail to attain something better. In other words, it is not so much that we cannot get clear; it is that we avoid doing so. By being honest with ourselves, we may think we will face something dreadful. We can also project fearfully that others will reject us or not cooperate with us if we define ourselves. Whether you are defining your personal needs and values or professional goals and practices, you will most assuredly not please everybody. By defining yourself clearly, you are making choices. You are telling yourself and others what you want, need, and expect. Therefore, you are choosing what is important to you. In getting clear and communicating clearly, your preferences, decisions, and choices will be known by and subject to the reactions of others.

It is the process of choosing that can frighten us so. We can feel exceedingly clear but still act as though we are uncertain because we may fear the consequences of making and communicating choices.

What if I lose an opportunity? What if people will not pay what I ask? What if I set a limit on what I will do and others reject my policies or take their business elsewhere? What if I get fired for stating what I am willing and not willing to do? What if my partner leaves me because I become assertive in what I need? What if others do not approve of what I want to do? What if no one wants to participate in something that is important to me? What if my boss doesn't agree that I deserve more money? What if I come across as harsh or immovable? What if I'm wrong and I discover it too late? What if this policy is a mistake? What if what I think I want is not actually what I need? What if I let go of an option and then someone else grabs it and I find out I should have taken it? What if.. What if.... What if.....? We can be ruled by our "what if" fears.

You can, however, challenge these fears. You can also ask yourself a different set of "what if" questions. What if I were to allow myself to go through the process of making choices, making mistakes and correcting them until I succeed? What if I discover how to really give to myself abundantly and let go of negative situations and people? What if I let go of some opportunities, because I cannot go after everything simultaneously, and accomplished my most important goals? What if I let others know what I was willing (and not willing) to do and they actually *liked or respected* what I had to say? What if people wanted to interact with me because they sensed my inner stability, confidence, and self-respect?

If we avoid getting clear, we only deprive ourselves of enjoying more of life's rewards. Simple wisdom tells us that self-respect cannot be gained by trying to be all things to all people. A sense of healthy independence cannot be gained by seeking the approval of others to be who we are. Inner peace cannot be gained by subverting what we know or even suspect to be the truth for us. Abundant living cannot be gained by playing small and staying confused to avoid threatening anyone who may react poorly to what we want, do, or say.

It takes courage to express what you know is right for you. This kind of independence can be quite scary. Others will react, negatively and positively. Either way it is a risk. We risk rejection or we risk changing. Both tend to bring up fear and anxiety. Yet, we can survive the anxiety and the fear of getting clear and communicating clearly. We have certainly survived the frustration and pain of ignoring ourselves. If fear was going to kill us, most of us would have been dead a thousand times by now. You may find out you are incorrect about certain choices and you will make mistakes. Good. Making mistakes is healthy and desirable. It is through making mistakes that we learn to better define our needs and care for ourselves.

If we express our desires directly and clearly and pursue them, all of us will experience, at times, negative results. However, we can adjust our efforts having gained more information, experience, and wisdom. This is logical thinking, but we are emotional and often irrational creatures and fall prey to the belief that mistakes and negative results will permanently hurt us. We may feel the need to brace ourselves against possible rejection and failure -- believing we will not survive disapproval or making mistakes. Negative results will happen to all of us and they do not feel good. The truth is that almost all of our negative experiences are merely distressing and are not permanent or dangerous. We can, then, regroup and try again. Even in cases where there has been intense suffering, there are individuals who choose to move on and up -- viewing their hardship as a way to learn to live differently and help others. It seems clear then that our fears and negative experiences, while upsetting, can be overcome. Getting clear means we will need to withstand the disappointments, errors and mistakes we make and try again until we prevail.

In being clear about preferences and decisions and pursuing them, we will often imagine both negative and positive outcomes coming out of our choices. This is quite human and understandable. As long as you also understand that your imaginings are like fortune-tellers and probably about as accurate. The point is you can survive both positive and negative outcomes. With the right perspective, you can face your projected fears of failure and success with the knowledge that you are born with basic resources that will, by necessity and invention, help you take care of yourself in either outcome. By being willing to deal with outcomes directly, you have succeeded before you have begun. The internal strength you will develop is far more important than any specific choice you make or goal you might attain.

If we cannot seem to get clear about some important issues in our lives, is it probably not confusion or ambivalence, but resistance. It may look like ambivalence, but is really a very sly way to keep ourselves from pursuing and having a more abundant life. Many of us may be living in a holding pattern -- wanting someone or something to come along and offer us the good things in life or to "just take care of us." Even so, many of us will move ahead despite this resistance. However, it can keep us living at a much lower level than we desire or is really acceptable.

This ambivalence or confusion can come up anytime something new is happening or if we get an inkling that we need to grow further or give something to ourselves. Resistance kicks in -- resistance to having what we need and going after it with a clear sense of purpose. This is when the internal arguments and rationalizations begin. If we can view our uncertainty as resistance to independence and abundance (not confusion or ambivalence), we can bear the discomfort of this process and move ahead. The rewards are well worth it. The greatest benefit is the internal strength we gain and the confidence that comes from knowing we can clearly discover and meet our own needs to a very great degree. In gaining this kind of independence, we will not be alone. In reality, we will attract others who will admire us, respect us, seek us out, or love us for our true selves.

We will always need to keep making choices, defining and redefining our personal and professional goals, wants, and needs, and giving to ourselves.

MAKING CLEAR REQUESTS

If you were to go to a real estate agent for a house or apartment, they would automatically start asking you questions about what you want. How much do you want to spend? What size are you looking for? What neighborhood? The answers are details. The details make up the picture of what you want. The agent could then envision this picture and contact you should they come across any possibilities for sale or rent. This example seems so simple and obvious. You are, with some prodding from the agent, getting clear and communicating clearly. The agent then, in turn (having gotten clear), talks to perspective owners and tells them clearly why you, the client, are a good prospect.

It is staggering how so many of us avoid this type of process because we will not face the discomfort of making choices and letting go of others. In looking for an apartment or house, we may respond: "I don't know how much I can spend. I don't know what size place I need. Anything that is big enough; I'd have to see it. I don't know if I need much closet space or not. If you tell me where you have something available, I'll think about whether that's a good neighborhood for me. What do you think would be good?" This would be giving an agent a ridiculously difficult task in keeping their minds open for something suitable to you, and it could irritate them.

Another example: "I'd like to meet a nice woman." What traits are you looking for? "I would like her to be breathing, and, oh yes, someone who will never ask me to be clear about what I want."

I had a client ask me to help him hire new employees but he refused to look at his finances to see what he could afford. Others ask what they should charge for their services but are afraid to call their colleagues to find out average industry rates. Many others want me to help them figure out how to pay back their debts without any information about how much money they need to live on. Others want to start a new business or service and want me to tell them what services I think they would like to offer. A number of individuals have asked me to help them with a career or job change, yet have not taken the time to really think about what they want or research any possibilities they might be interested in. They want the "magic" answer without taking a clear look.

The avoidance of getting clear is partly why clients come to me, and I have learned to be patient with these requests. With most of us, however, a lack of willingness to do some research, provide some information, or say what we want has a powerful effect. It frustrates almost everyone. It greatly impedes our ability to use others as a powerful resource for new opportunities. Others may view us as not serious about our needs and, therefore, will not be motivated to help us. In making requests, we do not have to know all the details of what we need. It would be enormously helpful, however, if we developed a willingness to approach the matter with a few details which are really important to us. This can make a world of difference in helping others help us move ahead.

CLARITY LIVES IN DETAILS

To move forward, begin by identifying some of the specific details in those areas you know you need to improve. Let go of any details you are uncertain about, for now. For example, you may know you need to get a computer to aid you in your work. Though you may not know how you will get a computer, you will be open to different solutions of getting one by clearly defining some of the things you need in a computer. Once you have gotten partially clear, research and get more specific information about the kind of computer and programs you need. Then, you will be able to communicate this to your computer knowledgeable friends or professionals. In this example, I have known many individuals who, once they knew what they needed, acquired used computers, were given a computer as a gift, obtained computers through barter, some received gifts from family to help pay for their computer, and others saved money until they could buy the computer they really wanted. In getting clear about even a few details of what you need, options and plans of action will emerge.

In another instance, if you know clearly that you need to work in a less hectic environment, open your mind to that possibility. Although you may not be clear about what other elements in a new work environment you require, you can focus on this one factor. By allowing yourself to inquire about new companies or situations that have a calmer environment, you will discover other elements (details) that are important to you as well. You may discover that you want to work with a smaller company, that does not force you to work overtime, and is closer to your home.

In getting clear about some of the details of your overall goals, it might be extremely helpful to write them down on paper. It gets your desires and wishes into tangible form. For each improvement or goal you know you want to achieve, outline it in writing. If you wish to try this, start with what you generally want. In other words, list the qualities and essence of a specific goal. Then make a "picture" of what you want by listing the details of what you need. Fill in as many details as you can that you know, *without question*, are important to you. Do not make up details that you are unsure of. If you are unsure of some of the specifics of your goal, as you start to take action more details will follow because you will naturally discover more about what you want. Also, it is a good idea to write on your list what is non-negotiable and negotiable to you. The aim in writing down your desires and goals this way is to focus your intentions and actions and motivate yourself. In becoming clear about your desires, you will create energy that attracts what you want. More often than not, getting focused in this way will help you achieve the essence and the actual non-negotiable aspects of your goals along with many of the negotiable (preferable) aspects as well.

After you have made your first list, you can think about it for a while and read it over a few times. You may find that you will naturally begin to communicate with others what you want and maybe even gently pursue it. You may want to carry what you have written with you. You can even use it as a check list when you begin to take actions toward what you need. If it is written you will not forget what is important to you -- as we can when we are anxious or emotional in pursuing an important goal. As you explore, it is important to keep in mind the following: If items listed on your written page are non-negotiable, make sure to view them as such. Do not bother exploring any situation that does not meet your non-negotiable items. This is very important. *Do not waste time when you know something is not right for you.* This would deprive yourself of the energy, time, and resources you need for situations that will meet your requirements. In giving yourself more abundance, you need to treat your most important desires with respect.

You will find that this kind of writing exercise can become a "divining rod" pointing you toward what you need. It certainly helps to keep you clear and focused. There are people who use this writing method to focus their efforts for all kinds of goals and desires such as apartments, jobs, material possessions, cities where they want to relocate and even to find lovers or mates. Try it. It works.

A replica of an actual list used by an individual to achieve an important goal is on the following page. (Figure A)

The individual who used this list had been looking for an apartment for weeks until he tried this approach. He kept the list out as he was making phone calls and knew he would not go to view any apartment that did not meet the essential requirements. After only one day of calling, he made only one appointment to view an apartment that seemed to be within the scope of what he wanted. He saw the apartment and took it on the spot. This apartment met every non-negotiable item on the list with the exception of good kitchen counter space. It also had hardwood floors, exposed brick

A New Apartment for me

I want a light, airy, warm apartment that I love coming home to and feel safe in.

Non-Negotiable

Must be $650.00 a month rent or less
Good closet space
Safe neighborhood
Elevator building
One Bedroom with separate door
Want to be lease-holder, not subtenant
No realty fee
Good kitchen counter space
Enough outlets for air-conditioner and appliances
Clean building with good maintenance records
Plenty of heat and hot water

Negotiable

Hard wood floors
Exposed brick walls
Security Doorman
Willing to "tip" super to get into building
Laundry in building
Good view

(Figure A)

walls in both the living room and the bedroom and the Super was tipped $200 to get into the building (a far cry from the normal $1,200 realty fee.) There was a 2 year lease at a $625.00 monthly rent ($25 below the $650 maximum which saved another $600 over the course of the lease) and there was a view of a garden. The security doorman, laundry and kitchen counter did not work out, but the new tenant was extremely happy and could easily accept the good fortune he had *defined for himself.* The rent for this apartment was considered "a steal" in a very competitive market in a city where vacancies for good apartments are thought to be extremely rare.

Again, you can use this simple method to define any goal, even in part, and continue to adjust the details as they become clear. You can write down a time by which you want to achieve a goal, but this should be a guide, not a commandment. You ARE NOT making a contract with yourself. Avoid saying to yourself that you *must* have this goal by this date. This would be an attempt to control your own human nature and the world around you (good luck), and it is a set up for failure. If you must, make a commitment to take an action or two a week until you find out if what you *think* you want is really what's best for you. Use the details as guidelines.

Perhaps you view outlining details as boring and tedious. Okay. At times, this is true. Nonetheless, being specific is part of the legwork we often need to do to make positive changes. Even when figuring out details takes painstaking effort, you can see it as setting up lights on a dark road that's leading you to a wonderful destination. When you have achieved your aim (or better), the efforts you have made at getting clear will have been well worth it.

LETTING GO OF HAVING TO KNOW IT ALL

One of the most common obstacles to moving in a positive direction is the notion that we must be clear about our entire approach and all of our plans *before* we take any action. If we cannot figure it all out in advance, then we remain stagnant and discouraged. This subtle insistence on having to know in advance the outcome and exact path to get a new job, make more money or find the right apartment or office space, etc., is one of the worst things we can do to ourselves. We deprive ourselves of moving ahead and learning as we go. We only need to proceed on one or two clear facts or desires. There may be fear in proceeding without knowing everything we need to do and how it will all turn out, but there is no obligation to make any important decision before we discover more of what we need. People can keep themselves from moving ahead for months and years until they "get it all straight in their heads," rather than act upon what they are clear about right now.

Do not deprive yourself in this manner. If you have found someone attractive, you might only need to be clear that they are single and open to a long-term relationship to have a date with them. Would you need to know *everything* about them just to go out and socialize? If so, you are only denying yourself the opportunity to find out more about *yourself* and what *you* need. If you are only willing to proceed based on past experiences, remember that this can only give you partial clarity about what to look for and how to proceed toward your goals. If you, the economy, the community, or the social environment has changed at all, you will need to learn to adjust your requirements to reach your goal. So, do not *pre-require* yourself to be clear about each aspect of your professional and personal goals before letting yourself move ahead. Your genuine desires and needs can only be discovered and met through allowing yourself to take action now and find out what will work for you in the long run. Start with a fact or two (or more) and explore. If exploration is difficult for you, take very small steps but take steps. You will survive the process of not knowing everything in advance. As you move ahead, you will proceed with more knowledge and wisdom. Through action, you will learn to define what is prosperous for you.

Do Not Judge Your Desires

Once you gain experience, or become clear about some of the details that seem to be important to you, do not judge whether your requirements are reasonable or unreasonable. If your requirements are not reasonable, the pattern of results you get in pursuing them will teach you how to adjust them as needed.

For instance, if you get clear that you want to hire an employee who will work 60 hours a week for $7 an hour, start asking and looking. (A client of mine found somebody who happily agreed to this -- a young man who wanted to save money for school.) If you want to move into a large, quiet apartment that has a great view, in a great neighborhood, yet want to spend 20% to 30% under market value, be open to getting it. Tell others clearly what you want and begin searching for it. (I am describing the apartment into which I recently moved. There is a security doorman in the lobby of the building and laundry room to boot.)

What you want and need is not wrong. If you cannot get it, remember that you will adapt to something that is close to what you need or better than you originally planned.

COMMUNICATING WITH OTHERS

Friends, colleagues, relatives, even acquaintances and strangers can be unlimited resources for helping you get what you want and attract what you need. Not every person in every instance will be of help. We may only need a few or even one solid contact. Get into the habit of clearly expressing what you are doing, what you want, and what you are looking for. You can make specific calls or arrange meetings to do this. You can also do this during casual conversation. At times, just by talking about what you want, you will find others offering help without you even asking them. Communicating clearly gets others thinking for you. The vast majority of us enjoy helping others succeed. Taking the risk to "put it out there" stimulates ourselves and others to see and explore new avenues.

Be straightforward in your discussions. Be specific when you know what you want and do not apologize. If you are afraid of being "politically incorrect," ask the person a little about their views before expressing yourself. You can also just be frank and not take on anyone's personal reaction to what you want.

There is no right or wrong to your desires. There is only that which helps you flourish. Be bold by acting as though you deserve to flourish by discovering, and expressing clearly, what you want. Whatever mistakes you make will teach you how to better approach the subject with the next person. Strength does not come from overpowering people. It comes by experiencing the rewards of putting yourself out there with clarity and seeing that it eventually works.

—❧— THE ONE-STOP SHOP HAD HIM STOPPED —❧—

Joseph, 35, was living alone in his parents' condominium in Westchester County, the suburbs of New York. They owned a house elsewhere. Joseph did not pay rent. The dependence on his mother and father was unhealthy by his own admission. Possessing a degree in Business, he had previously worked in the corporate world for several years. This had been an undesirable job and environment for him. He left and decided to pursue a career in supplemental health techniques (using meditation, body work, etc.) which he had always been interested in. Joseph's training put him more than $10,000.00 in debt. Once trained, he attempted to promote his services, and, in doing so, charged another $7,000 to his credit cards for professional equipment, promotion, etc. He was not earning much income from these newly acquired skills, and that is why he moved into his parents' apartment. He rented a small, inexpensive office in New York.

Joseph was trained in many areas and wanted to provide many services. Initially, he believed the more services he offered, the more clients he would attract. There were different pay rates for each service and services overlapped. He was confused about which services to focus on, however. Since he was confused, prospective clients, of course, were confused as well. Why would any client come to someone who did not seem to know how their business should be conducted or how to define their services? Joseph was avoiding getting clear about his wants and needs. He fell into the trap of focusing too heavily on what he thought the general public would accept. Since he had fear of making the wrong decisions and could not anticipate what would be acceptable to others, he made the mistake of trying to become a one-stop shop. In others words, out of fear, he was trying to be all things to all people, and kept himself quite confused. More months went by with much frustration and without much income. Joseph was anxious and discouraged and he felt panic about his growing debt.

—◇◇◇—

Joseph had the basic problem of assuming his genuine wants and needs might not get met. In so thinking, he automatically avoided getting clear about the services he wanted to perform and his professional requirements. He secretly judged his needs and requirements as unobtainable and possibly unacceptable. That is why he tried to offer so many different services and so many different prices. He was haphazardly trying to figure out what "they" needed, rather than concentrating on what he did best and promoting those services. By avoiding getting clear and communicating clearly to prospective clients, he actually delayed the process of finding out how to adjust his services or policies to maximum effect.

I immediately started working with him on the facts of his financial realities and ascertaining what he really wanted to do -- not what he thought might work. As we got clear about his financial picture and the types of services he wanted to perform, we were able to set priorities. These included dealing with his debt, creating income, establishing business policies and focusing on simplifying services. Though he was quite anxious in following my suggestions, within seven months of our work together, Joseph had gone from earning a few hundred dollars to a few thousand dollars monthly. He arranged for consolidation of his debt, making one affordable monthly payment. Establishing basic business policies such as standardized fees for the services he most enjoyed made a significant difference.

Joseph had been trying to "have something for everyone" believing this would attract more people. That may be effective if you are a big company with tremendous resources, but for one person it is usually creates great problems. Joseph was afraid he would lose clients if he defined his services and his policies in terms of what he wanted and needed. When he was willing to face this fear and get clear about his requirements, we were able to outline some basic business practices. He began, despite his apprehension, to communicate very simple policies clearly to prospective new clients and colleagues. He was able to take action because he did not wait to "know it all up front" (outline every aspect of his business) before communicating those decisions he was clear about. This basic clarity (and his perceived confidence) attracted more clients and his promotional efforts created more income. Once his business began to expand, Joseph adapted his services and policies as he discovered more clearly what both he and his clients needed.

Upon the conclusion of our work together, Joseph was getting clear about what he wanted in moving to an apartment of his own. Moving from his parents' apartment became a priority. He started making plans and saving money toward this end.

It was an exciting discovery for Joseph to find that he could attract clients for his unique services. Getting clear about his wants and needs and communicating them clearly gave him the renewed energy and positive disposition needed to exude a sense of confidence about himself and his work. Though he has much to learn, Joseph now has a sense of direction. His career became viable as he understood and practiced using clarity to help his business and help himself. Though getting clear and communicating clearly is a fearful process for many of us, Joseph discovered it was well worth the effort.

REMINDERS:

- You can overcome resistance to getting clear and learn to communicate what you need and want.

- You can plan to move ahead by defining only a few details of what you want.

- Write down the essential elements of your goals. They start to become real.

- Making mistakes is healthy and will teach you to adjust your efforts toward success.

- You do not need to know how things will work out before taking positive steps.

- You have the inner strength to withstand the reactions of others and the results of your choices.

- As you can begin to be open and direct about what you need, you begin to attract it.

- People can help you succeed when they know what you want.

SIMPLIFY YOUR CHOICES

CHAPTER 10

A man who tries to do everything, accomplishes nothing.
A Chinese proverb

In our modern social environment, we can easily get overwhelmed by the sheer amount of responsibilities and duties we need to perform on a daily basis. Priorities are difficult to establish because everything seems important. We cannot get to everything, of course, and in trying to keep up we may address some tasks haphazardly. Conversely, we can get so overwhelmed by the amount of choices before us that we do nothing, not knowing where to begin. Giving up and avoiding the complexity of making choices seems a lot easier. In either case, we do not seem to get very far. This leaves us with feelings of inadequacy, insecurity, and anger. Who would not be angered by frequently falling short? Who would not be angry with themselves for consistently being unable to decide and take action? A constant pressure of letting ourselves or others down can hang over us. Unfinished tasks and projects can create a sense of unending stress.

One of the most common forms of self-sabotage is simply trying to accomplish too much. Whether we learned it from our parents or adopted it from the popular culture, we overwhelm ourselves with more responsibilities than any human can possibly address. There are theories pointing to economic, social, and technological trends as the causes of the typically overly-stressed and/or immobilized person in our society. You could wait for external pressures to lift to relieve you of the burdens you experience. Chances are, however, you will need to change the way you approach things to make any substantial difference. Otherwise, you might be waiting for a few centuries or so for our productivity-obsessed society to operate at a more human pace for everyone.

GETTING UNPLUGGED

I have yet to observe anyone attaining greater success and emotional balance by intensely driving themselves every day. Yet, we do need to take action. To do so with any sanity, we might consider addressing our responsibilities and goals as a process, not an event. Speeding ahead creates greater stress and is contrary to abundant living.

Many clients come to me with initial complaints of severe busyness, to coin a term. Others complain of an inability to get started. Most everyone thinks they must do and do and do and do and do. It can be quite a challenge to try to convince someone they do not have to do so much.

If you put a dozen appliances in one electrical socket, nothing will work very well and you will blow a lot of fuses. We need to unplug some things. Overloading is a problem, but that is just what so many of us do in our lives -- plug in everything.

If you wish to enjoy greater abundance, consider simplifying your choices. This means putting some of your goals on the back burner. You do not necessarily have to eliminate them, just set them aside. If you are heading to a new destination and you are uncertain about the best course, you simplify your choices by trying one or two avenues. To repeat a thought from a previous chapter, you cannot be all things to all people. Being human, you cannot be all things at all times. You cannot *simultaneously* excel at being a parent, spouse, professional athlete, surgeon, professional accountant, lodge chairman, PTA member, Little League coach, cook, maid, community theater actor, political lobbyist, auxiliary police officer, and Sunday school teacher. It is odd how some of us point to working parents and their working spouses and herald their "superhuman" achievements with praise and admiration. Many of these same people go to bed exhausted and distressed and would give anything for six months away from it all. Isn't it nice that we think so highly of them? I am sure they would take time to appreciate it, if they were not in the middle of arranging meals, paying bills, doing housework, preparing for tomorrow's work load, making phones calls, and handling all family plans.

Whether we are truly overloaded or overwhelmed with what we are doing, or have great difficulty getting started, the answer is the same. We need to let go of some things. We need, metaphorically, to unplug some appliances so that others can work and the socket won't explode. Let go. There are others who can be the Little League coach today. Why not just attend the games? If you are an aspiring actor, is it time to lobby intensely for human rights, get married and have children? It is all a question of priorities and understanding that all things cannot be of equal value SIMULTANEOUSLY.

By making priorities and simplifying your choices, you are much more likely to accomplish your important goals. Then you may have the time and resources to devote to your delayed goals. You may even have decided that some of those delayed goals are not so important after all. We can operate under the false belief that we need to do everything at once to be more evolved as a person. When attempting to do this we are more likely to become totally self-involved, not giving much quality attention to any particular priority. We are then in jeopardy of not succeeding at anything at all. We need to unplug -- reduce or remove our energies toward some of our goals. If we do not simplify our choices, we may be condemning ourselves to a life where we are continually unsatisfied with any of our efforts.

Making Choices

Let us assume that this principle of simplifying choices is effective and that you are willing to slow down and simplify your options in order to become more prosperous. When you have reached a measure of success in focusing your energies differently, you can then address other goals with greater balance.

Even though this principle makes sense, you may still have some questions. What do you let go of right now? Which areas can wait? Of course, we all need to take care of our health, money, home, hygiene, and social commitments lest we become sick, in debt, out on the street and friendless. It does seem perplexing. However, the truth is it does not matter.

It does not matter whether you unplug the iron or the toaster.

Figure out which thing you need most and unplug the other one. Similarly, if going back to school is more important than renovating your apartment, then attend school and renovate your apartment as much as possible during school vacations. Do less with the apartment and spend less on it. If paying off your debt is more important than getting a new car, then pay your debt and put money away each week into a fund for a car until the debt is retired. The point is only you can figure out your priorities. If you simplify them (give them an order of value), your choices come more easily and you will succeed at your priorities, which almost invariably gives you the confidence and resources to succeed at the next goal.

CHOICES AND PEOPLE

Some of the most difficult choices become confusing because they involve family and friends. We regularly face choices involving our individual needs versus group (relationship) needs. Clearly, one choice does not have to be discarded for the other. However, if one choice gets more of your time, the other will logically get less. So, if relationships get more of your time and resources, your individual goals need to be fulfilled at a slower rate. Conversely, if you spend more time on individual pursuits, relationships will get less of your time. There is a balance to be struck, but you can learn to be honest about which is your natural inclination. If individual pursuits are extremely important, you may not make everyone happy, but human limitation dictates that you need to choose and let go of having the benefit of the other choice. Do not arbitrarily force yourself to be either career-oriented or relationship-oriented. Try to discover your true nature and go with it. Resist letting friends, family, and society dictate your basic nature. Discover it for yourself. Otherwise, you will suffer the consequences of trying to fully and simultaneously accomplish everything. Again, this can greatly hinder us, drain us, and keep us from succeeding at anything.

CHOICES AND TIME

A most troubling topic for many of us is time. Where should we spend our time? How much should we spend at each duty or goal?

As was previously stated, we need to give up the idea of accomplishing things *simultaneously*. We can focus on a few priorities, give some attention to others and put others still on the "delayed" list until our needs shift.

The amount of time we focus on a priority can be a few hours or days (e.g., paying bills, filing taxes, painting our room, cleaning the house). We can also focus on priorities that take years or the better part of a lifetime (becoming a doctor, raising children and seeing them off to college, traveling the world). Whatever our top priorities are, others will become less important. It is a simple fact that we need time to eat, sleep, work, and rest (even moderately). This time can only exist if we let go of pursuing all goals intensely and perfectly.

We can probably have most of what we want, but it is extremely doubtful if we will get it on an unrealistic and superhuman agenda.

~❧~ HE WAS DOING A LOT AND STANDING STILL ~❧~ HE SIMPLIFIED HIS CHOICES AND MOVED AHEAD

For the last ten years, Mark, 45, was working as a speech coach in Los Angeles. The last six of those years, he had been teaching at a professional trade school for radio broadcasting, and he had a small base of private clients as well. By his standards, Mark had been making a fairly good income in the late 1980's and early '90s of between $45 - $50 thousand annually. Yet, he longed to earn more money and gain greater recognition in his field. He frequently compared himself to others in his field who were "doing better," and he became frustrated with the lack of growth in his career. There was high regard for his work, but, with the high cost of urban living, his income level felt like it was becoming stagnant, without increases or long-term security. Work hours were long and intense. He was routinely tired and worn out. On his own, Mark found a corporate client. Though he began to make a bit more money, his schedule became even more hectic. A professional acquaintance told him I might be able to help.

—◇◇◇—

Over the course of our first few telephone conferences, Mark told me of his other goals besides the things he was already pursuing. Listening to the list made my head swim. He wanted to continue teaching, get more corporate clients, get jobs coaching for films and tv programs, perform in television and radio voice-overs, work as an actor in films and television himself, be the speech coach for national broadcast personalities and politicians, begin a full exercise program, move out of the metropolitan area, have more time for social engagements, and produce tapes and video cassettes for sale. Whew! Mark wanted to make more money in less time so he could move toward these other objectives. It's not that his desires were wrong. It's just that he wanted to, and thought he should, work on all of these things at the same time.

I assured him that it was possible to make a good deal more money in less time. I told him he would probably need to give up some of his other objectives for the time being. They were keeping him blocked, even though he was not acting on the majority of them. This explanation seemed odd to him. However, at the beginning of working with him, I knew if Mark got more free time he would only fill it up again and keep himself from making substantial progress with anything. Overwhelming himself with work and activities was clearly a pattern for him.

Mark finally accepted the idea that only by "unplugging" some of his wants, even temporarily, could he move forward on his most important goals of making more money and having more personal time. Though he had strong impulses to talk about and pursue a number of different goals, I kept guiding him back to keeping his efforts uncomplicated. He became willing to simplify his current circumstances without acting on those impulses. This was difficult for him but it paid off. It took a little more than a year, but he raised his corporate rates and took more time off. He cut back his private clients to a few hours a week and simplified his schedule to teaching only twice a week. I helped Mark raise his corporate fees more than 100%. With little effort on his part, he was getting quite a good reputation with his corporate clients and his name was being referred to other companies and individual celebrities. Upon the conclusion of our work together, Mark was working nearly 25% fewer hours while his total income doubled. Since he had more time, he took some acting classes, developed a love relationship, and found time to exercise. Mark took two luxurious vacations during the year and bought a better car.

During our last few phone sessions, we examined investing his savings -- which had grown substantially -- and discussed his other career goals. I reminded him that it was possible to attain any of his other goals if he was willing to go through the process of choosing priorities and delaying other less important goals. I was hopeful that Mark's successes with letting go and placing some of his desires on hold convinced him of the soundness of simplifying his choices.

REMINDERS:

- Let go of pursuing too many goals and responsibilities simultaneously.

- The greatest chance for success <u>and</u> emotional balance lies in your willingness to simplify your choices and efforts.

- By choosing priorities, you can make it easier to decide how to spend your time and energy.

- In delaying certain desires and making choices, other options are set aside, not eliminated.

- You do not have to wait for external pressures to lift to simplify your life.

- Stay true to your nature and follow your strongest desires.

Give Yourself a Raise

Stay in Current Reality

CHAPTER 11

> *Yes, I want to hear the truth, but I don't want*
> *to deal with the facts!*
> Statement by a new client

It is vital to take a clear and accurate view of our present circumstances. If we can look squarely and honestly at the facts, we give ourselves the ability to improve our situation much more readily. Why? Because all decisions and plans we make will come from our view of these facts. Through the filter of our emotions, we are apt to misinterpret our situation. It is easy to review the past with blame and regret and preview the future with anxious anticipation. This colors our perspective tremendously.

One of my clients came to me complaining that his cash flow was "killing him." When asked about his income, expenses and savings, it was revealed that he was giving his nephew several hundred dollars a month out of an excessive sense of duty. It also became clear his nephew had other resources for money. Furthermore, this client had over $350,000 in investments and liquid assets, a good credit rating, and no outstanding debts. Yet, he thought he was broke because his weekly expenses were equal to his weekly salary. Most of us would probably find his viewpoint absurd, but it felt true to him. We can all recount stories where a person's present circumstances are better than they view them. We can also recount tales of individuals who avoid the facts of their situation and are in more trouble than they seem aware of. This makes the point that our emotions can create denial that blocks clear thinking.

Separating Feelings From Facts

We may *feel* like we are in a crisis. That does not mean we *are* in one. When we are in an emotional state, we are rarely the best judges of our circumstances. We may need the help of a calm person who can help us assess our situation.

There is nothing wrong with feelings. They can be powerful messages to ourselves. We can, however, learn to act, or refrain from acting, based on facts (current reality), not feelings. It is by being willing to live in the present that allows us to make decisions that will lead to a more rewarding future.

Almost certainly, we will need to slow ourselves down. Though we may feel an urgent need to make drastic changes, we can act with patience and persistence based on a realistic view of our circumstances. This gives us the optimum chance of succeeding. On the other hand, when a clear and reliable view of our situation shows a need for swift action, we do not kid ourselves that everything is okay. To the best of our ability and with as much courage as possible, we need to face facts. We may not know what to do with these facts once we take a square look at them, but just knowing them gives us a chance to address them at some point. If we avoid facing our real circumstances, we can set ourselves up for much harm to our physical, financial, and emotional well-being.

The Illusion of the Quick Fix

There are many motivational and financial pundits who espouse a "quick-fix" mentality. There is one who says you can change your life in 30 days by following his techniques and ideas. This person has made millions of dollars with books and tapes promoting his methods. That is fine. He is increasing his prosperity. The question is: Would you be increasing yours trying to turn your reality around in 30 days? By his own admission, this individual developed and practiced different techniques for years and read over 400 books on subjects related to human potential. He took time to assimilate this knowledge and wisdom. He took time to integrate these philosophies into his own life. It is true he had a spurt of success in a year or more, after years of diligence that finally clicked inside him. Yet, he says you do not have to improve with patient persistence over time. Your life can turn around in 30 days, and your increased power will bring you what you want in a matter of weeks or months. Great idea -- if you are among the very small percentage of those who may be able to do that. Or you may be one of the countless millions, if not billions, of human beings, like myself, who need to assimilate change.

We are all human. So, each of us, at times, feels an urgent need to change rapidly. Who wants to bear the discomfort that comes with moderate and consistent change? We need, however, to examine and check the feelings of "emergency" and bring them into perspective. We also need to understand the nature of change. If we fight the fact that change needs to be assimilated and is a process, not an event, we end up discouraged and drained after the initial motivation wears off or find ourselves naturally procrastinating in reaction to having to do so much so quickly.

Could you run a marathon after only 30 days of beginning exercise? Could you take a luxurious vacation for two weeks to an exotic destination after only 30 days of saving money from your paycheck? Obviously, the answer is no. What we could do is open our minds to doing things differently in 30 days and begin the process of dealing with our feelings of urgency. In this way, we can plan to run a marathon and plan to save and take our vacation. If the motivational consultant in question would say, "You can open your mind much more in 30 days," many more of us could possibly do that.

We change the circumstances of our lives by consistent, not instant, efforts. We move forward by adopting new philosophies and beliefs and developing new habits over time. We can separate our feelings from facts and become willing to try new ways that have a genuine chance of working. Quick fixes inspired by stirred up emotions are temporary, illusory, and often set us back further after the initial promise of quick change wears off.

LOOKING AT THE NUMBERS

How then do we separate facts from feelings? One important step in living more abundantly is looking at the numbers (your finances) clearly.

The title of this book certainly provokes images of more money, and stories of increased income are in this book, so we can assume this has brought the issue of your finances to your mind. Therefore, an accurate assessment of your money situation is one of the most effective means for making plans to move ahead. I have gone over the finances of almost every client with whom I have worked. This has not always been easy. Getting clear and talking clearly about money issues can stir strong emotions. There are people who would rather discuss the intimate details of their sex lives than clearly disclose financial facts or their thoughts (and secrets) about their money situation. Though so many of us have been taught to keep our finances private, you do not become abundant by staying in total secrecy. Taking the chance to get clear about your finances, and trusting someone with the real facts of your money situation, can be an extremely effective method in growing beyond fears around money and becoming more prosperous. This can be a powerful step in deciding how you want to proceed toward your goals. Often, the facts lead to decisions so obvious the choices almost make themselves.

Dealing with Fear of Financial Clarity

The problem with looking at financial facts is the apprehension that may come from even thinking about this information -- let alone sitting down to do it. We think we will discover something terrible and have to make decisions or take swift actions for which we are unprepared. Nothing could be further from the truth. All you need to do is be willing to look at your financial situation as accurately as possible. That is all. There is nothing you need do beyond that. Just by looking clearly at something, you begin an internal and subconscious process of problem solving. You do not need to fret about the facts. (Not that I would dissuade you from your God given right to worry needlessly, as we all do!) In those extremely rare instances where swift action is called for, you will give yourself the gift of being able to act with clarity.

In coming to financial clarity, the facts may stimulate your mind to come up with alternatives you never considered. Or, you may find you want help with something you previously (subconsciously) have ignored. To make a metaphor, it would be better to know now you have a cavity in a tooth than to wait until you need to get a root canal. Knowledge gives you options and can lead to inspiration, invention, and creative solutions. Any initial fear of looking at your situation will be outweighed by the forward movement that comes from your willingness to be honest and clear.

If the idea of sitting down with pad and pen and calculating numbers is too upsetting or frightening for you, do not despair. First, do not criticize yourself for this. Money vagueness and avoidance of getting clear around finances is very common. Some of us may have irregular and erratic forms of income and expenses which make it difficult to come up with an accurate financial picture. Others simply get confused by mathematics. However, vagueness can also come from fearful, and even phobic, anticipation of taking responsibility for handling money and staying clear about numbers and finances. If you face facts squarely, they may point to changes you need to make but do not want to face. For many of us, it would be anxiety-provoking to know this information. This is why it is suggested not to do anything at first about the facts you find.

If any of the above circumstances apply to you, do not figure out your finances alone. The method of calculating your finances that follows is focused on helping you look at the pattern of your earning and spending habits. It is meant to aid you in getting clear, giving you more options based on facts, or to help motivate you to find solutions -- not send you into panic. If you need to, find a friend or hire someone to help you who can be clear, calm and patient while they sit with you and go over your numbers. Then do it.

If you need to bypass calculating your finances for now, so be it. No shame. No blame. There is a lot more in this book to aid you in thinking more prosperously and living more abundantly. Do not absolutely force yourself to do this. When you are ready, however, you can come back to this section. Taking an honest look at your financial situation is a healthy thing to do. Just be sure to do it with all the support you need.

THE ELEMENTS OF YOUR FINANCIAL PICTURE

Whether you have gone over your finances recently or not, it would be useful to presently calculate your revenues, expenses and your overall financial picture. The purpose, again, is to simply make a realistic assessment of the facts. Let us start by defining revenue and assets.

INCOME

Any money that comes to you regularly as a form of payment, for any reason, that is available for you to spend (e.g., salary, royalties, business/self-employment income, interest on investments, dividends, regular gifts of money).

SAVINGS
Money in any accounts, funds, shoe boxes, mattresses, etc., that you can withdraw immediately to use for expenses and that you keep for specific purposes. This means that your savings are meant to be spent. This is different than investments, which are for long-term security.

INVESTMENTS
Money set aside in the form of stocks and bonds, or deposited in cd's, retirement/pension funds, etc., that you could use, if necessary, for expenses. The total amount of the investment is not the amount to calculate; it is the amount you can get as cash that is important. If you receive dividend or interest payments from your investments, that is income. The principal, or portion remaining that is available as cash if you liquidate (withdraw it), is your investment.

PROPERTY
Anything you **can sell or take a collateralized loan against** in an emergency. This includes a house, condominium, car, jewelry, antiques, books, rugs, equipment, baseball cards -- anything at all. You determine the value by getting an appraisal of the cash sale value (not insurance replacement value) of the item.

OTHER RESOURCES
Money you **could borrow** on an unsecured or secured basis **without pressure of having to pay it back quickly.** Typically, this would be loans from relatives or friends. (If it's a lover, beware as this can really put intense stress on a relationship.) Other resources do *not* include credit cards, unsecured bank loans, or any other unsecured debt. Taking out unsecured loans from financial organizations (without having to provide collateral) sets you up for financial crisis and disaster unless you can clearly afford monthly payments. The ability to make such payments needs to be based on facts, not speculation, potential income, or wishful thinking. Otherwise, you will be living in chronic debt which erodes confidence and any efforts to become more prosperous.

Give Yourself a Raise

Let us now define expenses.

EXPENSES
Any money you spend or payments you make to maintain your life. If you have certain payments automatically deducted from a paycheck, such as insurance premiums, alimony, garnishments -- these are also expenses. You will have both fixed expenses, such as rent and car payments, and variable expenses, such as groceries, clothing, and repair bills. More will follow on how to calculate these different kinds of expenditures.

Here is a partial list of spending categories you may want to refer to later. Each individual can have a variety of other expenses that are not listed here.

Rent/Mortgage	Dining Out
Utilities	Car & Medical Insurance
Groceries	Transportation
Telephone	Entertainment/Recreation
Household Supplies	Property/Income Taxes
Appliances	Pet Expenses
Haircuts/Grooming	Gifts/Holiday Expenses
Clothing	Charitable Donations
Cable TV	Furniture
Gym Membership	Banking Fees
Postage/Stationery	Home Decorations
Medical Expenses	Union Dues
Car/Home Repairs	Dental Expenses
Counselling Services	Laundry/Dry Cleaning
Debt Repayment	Music Purchases
Trips/Vacations	Papers/Books/Magazines
Tips/Gratuities	Alimony/Child Support
Legal Fees	Miscellaneous (Unexpected)

INCOME TAXES
If you have enough payroll taxes regularly taken out of your paycheck so that you do not owe the government additional money at the end of the year, there is no need to worry. However, if you generally must send the federal or state government additional taxes,

you should list this as an additional expense. If this is the case, or if you are legally required to pay estimated income taxes from your reported business or self-employment income, keep in mind *you need to make an expense category for these taxes and pay them.*

Some words to those with tax problems: if you are not paying taxes and you are using the money to get by with living expenses or for other purposes, the government will not just forget about you. This is a certainty. The penalties and interest you accrue can add up to double, triple and quadruple your debt. This is not meant to scare you. This is the reality. If you do not deal with taxes responsibly (file them, contact tax agencies to make some attempt at payment or deferment), you will pay a heavier price down the road. If you avoid this issue, eventually, income tax agencies will find you, get tough with you, seize bank accounts and assets, and seriously undermine your efforts to move ahead and become more prosperous. Yet, there is no need to panic. Be willing to address tax issues at soon as you can. It would be better if you did so voluntarily (getting all the help you need) rather than wait indefinitely and suffer greater consequences. (See Section III, page 166, "Face Your Tax Debt.")

*(**Note to all:** You <u>can</u> live abundantly on the money you receive after paying your taxes. Yes, without a doubt, millions and maybe even billions of tax dollars are squandered. But remember, taxes also go to expenses for police, firemen, building and repairing roads, public education, libraries, grants to research cures for serious illnesses, and emergency services just to name a few. Take your deductions, as aggressively as is appropriate, but know that you are paying tax dollars, at least in part, for your own well-being.)*

Calculating Your Income

To get clear about the current reality of your financial picture, let us now calculate your **monthly average net income**. Do this by listing and/or adding all sources of your gross income. If you receive a paycheck from which taxes are automatically taken out and it covers your tax liability, just list the net amount. If you have money automatically taken out of your paycheck for specific expenses or that goes to bank accounts of any kind, add back in these miscellaneous payments to get your real net income. For example: if your net pay is $650.00 every two weeks but $25 is automatically taken out for insurance, $30 for dues and $100 goes to a savings account, add back the $155 total to get your actual net income of $805 every two weeks. Then list these deducted items as expenses later on. Why? You may decide to alter these deductions once you assess your total financial picture.

If you receive income for which taxes are not withdrawn for you, deduct a percentage of the total. For example, if you made $4,000 last month and your tax liability is approximately 25%, then your probable taxes for that month would be $1,000 and your net income is $3,000. Your accountant or tax preparer should be able to give you a close approximation of the percentage you pay for every dollar you earn in non-taxed income or dividend payments. If you had income from more than one source, add the totals together to calculate your total net income for the month. Round off your figures to whole dollars. Copy the simple form below onto another piece of paper and calculate your numbers for last month.

Salary Income:

Check Totals .... $ _____
Add back Misc. Deductions .... $ _____
Net Income .... $ _____

Freelance/Business/Non-Employee Revenue

Gross .... $ _____
Less (__%) Tax on Gross .... $ _____
Net Income .... $ _____

Average Monthly Dividend Income/Regular Gifts
of Money that are taxable:

Gross .... $ _____
Less (__%) Tax on Gross .... $ _____
Net Income .... $ _____

NET INCOME FOR MONTH .... $ _____

Do your income calculations for the most recent three full calendar months -- six months is even better. Take the total of all these months and divide by the number of months to get your **average monthly net income**.

Average Monthly Net Income
_____

Net Income from Month 1 .... $ _____
Net Income from Month 2 ....   _____
Net Income from Month 3 ....   _____
_____

TOTAL FOR 3 MONTHS............. $ _____

AVERAGE (Total divided by 3) ..... $ _____

(**Note:** If you are a sole proprietor, freelance professional or business owner and do not pay yourself a regular salary, you need to categorize and subtract your average monthly business expenses from your *monthly gross revenue* to get your *gross profit*. Estimated taxes are then deducted from your *gross profit* to determine your *net income*. First, calculate your personal expenses as outlined under the next heading. Then go back and do the same thing for your business expenses.)

CALCULATE YOUR EXPENSES

Next, calculate your **average monthly expenses**. You do not need to do this in one sitting. Go as slowly as you need, take as many sessions over as many days as you need to complete the process. Remember, accuracy and the willingness to look at your numbers counts -- not speed. Even if you can only get ballpark figures, it will help you understand more of what you need to do in handling your finances and your life.

Expenses will be calculated in four steps. Get a notebook or four sheets of lined paper and write a separate heading on a separate page for each of these expense areas: (1) Fixed Monthly Expenses, (2) Variable Living Expenses, (3) Fixed Periodic Expenses, and (4) Variable Periodic Expenses. Refer to your records (including receipts, checkbooks, ledgers) to find the amounts needed. Make educated estimates of those expenses for which you do not keep records. If you need it, ask for help to make these estimates. You can list your totals in pencil (as they may change) on a form like the one below.

PAGE 1

Fixed Monthly Expenses	
Mortgage (Rent)	$ 800
Medical Insurance	$ 250
School Loan	$ 123
Utilities	$ 50
Telephone	$ 75
Credit Card Payments	$ 100
Cable TV Service	$ 30
TOTAL	$1428

Page 1: Fixed Monthly Expenses

List *monthly payments that do not widely vary*. Rent, mortgage, insurance premiums, cable TV bills, loan payments, etc. and add them up. Average your monthly bills, phone, electric bills, etc. and list them with your fixed expenses. Credit card payments should be listed here. (If your credit card or other debt repayments vary greatly, refer to Section III, page 162, "Standardizing Your Credit Card and Other Debt Repayments.")

To begin, draw a line down the center of the page and list every expense amount next to each category. Refer back to the list earlier in this chapter for category ideas. You may wish to purchase a home budget book or financial record-keeping materials at your local stationery or office supply store to give you more expense category ideas.

Page 2: Variable Living Expenses

List **day-to-day living expenses** for one week such as groceries, dining at restaurants, transportation, gasoline, magazines/newspapers, house supplies, and any items you use for daily living. If you do not keep records (and you may seriously wish to start if you are going to make effective financial decisions), calculate each category by estimating your cost per week for that expense. Then, multiply each category by 52 (weeks) and divide by 12 (months). For example: Groceries $90 per week MULTIPLY by 52 (weeks) = $4,680 DIVIDED by 12 (months) = $390 average per month. In some cases, you may wish to use monthly estimates for less frequent categories such as postage and entertainment. Add all of your average monthly expenses in each category together to get your total variable living expenses on average for the month.

Page 3:   Fixed Periodic Expenses

List payments you make that are **regular but are paid less frequently than once a month** (such as quarterly, semi-annually or annually). These expenses might include property taxes, car insurance, membership fees, union dues, accounting fees. Take the total payment due and divide by the number of months it covers. Typically, this means you will be dividing yearly payments by 12 (months) and quarterly payments by 3 (months). Again, you want to find the monthly average.

Page 4:   Variable Periodic Expenses

This may be more difficult to figure out, but do your best to estimate how much you spend on vacations/trips, occasional medical expenses, clothes, holiday expenses and gifts, birthdays and celebrations, special one time purchases of equipment or furniture that you buy or intend to buy, other one-time expenses that are planned for, etc., for the entire year. List the total amount of these expenses and divide by 12 (months). Also, put in an amount for a miscellaneous expense category. Inevitably surprise expenses crop up such as car and home repairs, supplies, unforeseen medical or dental expenses, etc. Do not leave this category out of your calculations. These are the *unexpected* items that can create havoc with your finances. (If you charge any of these items then add an appropriate amount to your monthly credit card payment to cover any of the expenses on this page.)

CALCULATING YOUR MONTHLY PROFIT/LOSS

Now, using a photocopy or your own version of the form below, list your monthly net income for the last three months and your calculated Average Monthly Income. Next, add your expenses together. List the subtotal from each page and add them together to get your total Average Monthly expenses. Finally, subtract your total Average Monthly Expenses from your Average Monthly Income to get your Average Monthly Profit or loss.

AVERAGE MONTHLY PROFIT (LOSS)

NET INCOME (After actual or estimated taxes deducted)

Month of _____ .... $ _____
Month of _____ ....   _____
Month of _____ ....   _____
TOTAL .... $ _____
(A) AVERAGE (Total divided by 3) ...... $ _____

EXPENSES (List subtotal from each separate Page 1-4)

Fixed Monthly - Page 1 .... $ _____
Variable Living - Page 2 ....   _____
Fixed Periodic - Page 3 ....   _____
Variable Periodic - Page 4 ....   _____
(B) TOTAL EXPENSES .... $ _____

MONTHLY PROFIT (LOSS)

Average Income (from Line A) .... $ _____
Average Expenses (from Line B) ....   _____
PROFIT (LOSS) (A minus B) .... $ _____

If you have made it this far, good work! Calculating these figures will give you an immediate picture of your financial situation. Remember, you are just taking a look. You should be able to see, on average, how much profit or loss you are operating at each month. If you are currently operating at a monthly profit, you can make decisions to increase your expenses, save money, take a trip, or the like. Thoughtfully discuss your options with someone you can trust. You may wish to make plans to pursue a vision or make an important investment in your life.

If you are operating at a loss, then you need to turn to your assets (if you have any) to see how long you can continue to operate at a loss. If you are operating at a loss and have no savings, investments or property of any kind, then you need to look at these figures and accept the situation for the moment. You may feel upset or frightened, but that is better than denying that you can continue to earn less than you need or extravagantly overspend. You may need additional assistance which will be discussed shortly. (If you have absolutely no assets, read the suggestion under the next heading on the assumption that at some point you will.)

Calculating Your Assets

If you are operating at a loss and have savings, investments or property, calculate their immediate cash value. If you do not know the cash value of something, approximate it conservatively and then find out at some point what its cash value really is. Be careful with personal items, assessing them for cash, not for insurance appraisal value. Until you can earn more money or control unnecessary compulsive spending, you may need to use these assets to cover your losses. Please seek sound advice before doing this. Otherwise, you may find yourself covering losses and using up all your assets without having addressed the underlying problems of underearning or overspending. Still, it is helpful to total the cash value of all your assets as it can give you options and even calm you down by showing you that there is time to deal with your financial situation.

Keep in mind that cutting expenses only works if such expenses are incurred extravagantly and impulsively, for example, excessive shopping for clothes or other goods, impromptu trips, buying gifts frequently, too much spontaneous socializing expenses, and use of credit cards to "treat yourself." Conversely, depriving yourself of necessary items and expenditures (even planned entertainment and leisure expenses) is self-defeating and prolongs your money problems. Even if you must cut back in some categories for the moment, commit to having more money for those categories as soon as you can. Keep all categories open in your mind *and* list them on paper even if the amount you are spending in any category is momentarily zero. This keeps space in your thinking and attitude for money to flow into these categories in the future.

If your assets give you a one, two, or three month cushion to cover your average monthly loss, you could react in at least two ways. You could feel panic at having <u>only</u> a few months. Or, you could feel relieved at having <u>at least</u> a few months to find new ways of earning more money. Any reaction you have comes from your beliefs and your viewpoint. The Current Reality of the situation, however, is that *you are fine for right now.*

What to Do Now

You do not need, at this point, to calculate Other Assets (loans from family and friends), unless you are in a true emergency. This means homelessness or the like. Refrain from going to Other Assets unless you know it is *absolutely your only legal alternative to stay afloat.* Remember, an urgent feeling does not mean an actual emergency, and having both emotional and financial ties to the same person creates a dependence that is contrary to self-sufficiency and personal prosperity. If necessary, do it, but for the sake of trying to become financially independent and prosperous do not include family money as possible income for yourself if you have assets of your own.

Your only job in looking at the numbers is to stimulate your mind. If your numbers look good, you do not need to go on a spending spree. A well thought out and more abundant plan for spending is called for, or contemplation of pursuing a long held dream. If your situation looks difficult, this does not mean you need to go into frantic action. It means you stay clearly in the present and refrain from acting impulsively. We do not need to allow ourselves to get into false projections of fear or insecurity. You have, after all, survived and coped until now. *Despite what you may feel,* you can plan to take actions based on the present circumstances that, in most cases, do not suggest drastic measures.

If you operate out of fear, denial, or urgency, you will set yourself up for problems. It is not suggested you ignore any feelings of anxiety your situation may evoke. You may wish to talk to an understanding person about them. Reassure yourself that you have the ability to adapt. Remind yourself continuously that you can learn to plan, decide, and act to move toward increasing your prosperity. If you can learn, you can change in a positive direction. To act out of fear can become a self-fulfilling prophesy.

This exercise in Current Reality may also demonstrate to you that you no longer need to accept a depriving situation. It may also tell you to take swift action before legal procedures or other problems arise. At the very least, it probably will motivate you in some way. In being willing to look at your current situation accurately, you give yourself the opportunity to let your resourcefulness become awakened and go to work, even if by necessity.

If you are having difficulty assessing your financial circumstances, again, seek the help of a trusted person who is good with numbers. Look for an individual who will keep what you convey in confidence and who can offer you calm guidance. Even if it is only one person who knows your circumstances, it may be extremely helpful in making decisions and can bring you much relief to let someone know the details of your money situation and your thoughts and feelings around it. Such an individual needs to help you assess the facts of your circumstances without judging or taking advantage of you. If you need to, hire a professional who understands these financial issues and *who is not an alarmist*. If you begin to confide in someone who reacts in an anxious or judgmental way to your financial situation, do not continue to discuss the issue with that individual -- even if they are your spouse. Seek a different person, and keep looking until you can find someone who can provide the support you need.

Go to the library or bookstore and find a book or two on the subject of personal finances or getting out of debt. One of the best is How to Get Out of Debt, Stay Out of Debt and Live Prosperously written by Jerrold Mundis and published by Bantam Books. Another is Money is My Friend by Phil Laut and published by Ballantine Books (as Ivy Books). These and other books offer advice regarding pressing money issues in greater detail than can be covered here. Other perspectives that espouse prosperity thinking and abundant living can only help reinforce the ideas presented here.

Make a practice of calculating and looking at your numbers regularly -- every three months is a good rule of thumb. The time it takes to do this is well worth the clarity, insight, and motivation it can give you by doing so. As you become and continue to stay clear, you will talk to someone you can trust about what to do.

Money Vagueness, Problem Debting, Problem Spending, Underearning

If you have skipped the last subsection dealing with numbers or have problems dealing with money, you may be someone who cannot seem to get clear about their financial circumstances. Numbers might scare you and you may feel like you cannot make sense of them. You may need additional support. If you are in constant and overwhelming debt through credit cards, taxes, unpaid bills or loans, you may have a compulsive problem with debt. If you are consistently spending more than you make even when your income increases, you may have a compulsive spending habit. Conversely, you may have great difficulty spending money on yourself when you have it. If you are constantly in situations where you never earn enough to meet your expenses, chances are you are an underearner. If you have little money and are in severe crisis, with no savings, no immediate resources, and often turn to your family and friends for money, you may have a financial dependency problem. All these cases stem from the same core problem. You may be suffering from compulsive or uncontrolled self-deprivation.

Our internal mechanism for self-sabotage may be so strong that we cannot get ahead with money or our careers, no matter how we try. If this your situation, it is probable that you need more assistance and information than can be provided here.

Besides the book by Mr. Mundis listed above, there are other ways to get help (see Resources section). One way to get assistance is to contact Debtors Anonymous (DA), a self-help organization, that focuses on aiding individuals who deprive themselves financially. There are groups throughout the U.S. and a few in Canada. You can find them in your local phone book, or call directory assistance of major cities nearest you to get information or obtain a meeting list.

If you cannot find a group by these means, write to The General Service Board of Debtors Anonymous, P.O. Box 400, New York, NY 10163 for more information. You may call them at (212) 642-8220. They have helped thousands of individuals with chronic and overwhelming financial issues.

BEARING DISCOMFORT

If we are to stay in Current Reality, it is likely we will feel some discomfort. In some cases, there will be extreme anxiety and frustration. It can be quite difficult to accept the facts of our circumstances without knowing exactly how to improve them.

Bearing discomfort means adopting the mental attitude that we can face, survive and move beyond our current situations. We can learn to accept that we will need to change some things *before* we move on. Bearing discomfort means becoming willing to let ourselves feel emotionally uncomfortable yet not act impulsively to "fix" the problem. If we are to make progress, we need to persist steadily by trying to alter our perspective and take appropriate actions at a pace that does not overwhelm us. It means we do not race ahead or delay. This is a simple idea but hardly easy.

You, like most of us, may need a new philosophy so that you can withstand the thoughts and feelings that come with facing facts objectively. You must keep your sights on what you need to do in the present to move yourself to the very next step. To help yourself do this, consider the idea of bearing the discomfort of your Current Reality. Consider that you may need to move slowly ahead through any resistance that may arise. If you are a person who does not experience resistance or fear to a great degree, you are blessed. If you are a person whose resistance and fear of change are formidable, then adopt the attitude that you are willing to face discomfort. You do not need to be a saint or martyr, but you may find bearing some discomfort and anxiety health-engendering and stamina building. You would be doing so for an extremely good cause, namely, your own contentment and prosperity. This can carry you through many difficulties.

There is a great difference between experiencing the pain of procrastination and self-deprivation and experiencing the growing pains of facing reality and making the necessary shifts to alter your future for the better. One keeps us stuck in an unrelenting state of boredom, frustration, and despair. The other gives us the mechanism by which we will attain greater self-discipline, self-respect, and self-fulfillment.

—❧— SHE TURNED PANIC INTO PROGRESS —❧—

June, a computer software analyst was fired from her job and came to me through a reference. There had been no work for her in more than eight months, and she had been on several interviews without success. To aid her job search, June's former employer had provided the services of an out placement firm (a company that provides phones, fax machines, and guidance to help unemployed executives secure new employment). She had no tangible results with this resource. Eventually, June moved in with relatives in Montclair, New Jersey (40 minutes from Manhattan) to defray her living expenses as she had only unemployment payments to support her. A young daughter resided with her estranged husband, and June did not enjoy much influence with the raising of her child. Unable to afford an attorney, June suffered poor visitation rights. It was just as well, in her mind, that she did not have custody of a child she could not provide for. Her soon-to-be ex-husband did not have the means to provide temporary or long-term alimony.

June was desperate for work and, by living with relatives at the age of 34, her esteem was taking a beating. Before she was fired, June was making $65,000 annually. At the point she came to me, June was working hard to get a consulting job paying only $500 a week. Someone with her expertise should have earned a minimum of $1,000 weekly in the same situation. Obtaining this job was uncertain. It was out-of-town and of indefinite duration. June believed she needed money immediately and had to take any opportunity at this low point in her life.

—◇◇◇—

Despite her fears, I convinced June that working out-of-town in an uncertain situation for one-half of normal wages was self-defeating. June had a difficult time believing my assessment because she was falling into the common trap of accepting an underearning situation to create potential income. June needed to shift her thinking and perspective. She was having urgent feelings, but she was not in an urgent situation. We calculated her finances, and June came to understand that while her current reality was not pleasant, it was not a crisis. She had enough money to live on and pay basic expenses. Though she did not want to stay in her present situation a long time, she, in fact, had time. There was no financial or physical reason she needed to rush into any job. At times, she wanted both to give up and alternately race ahead to do anything. When we continued to take a realistic view of her circumstances, June agreed to stay with her relatives and look for a _good_ job, rather than just any job. To say the least, this was not comfortable.

For months, June continued her job search very diligently but without success. She became very disenchanted with the corporate interview process. She went on these interviews thinking she should work in a corporation because she needed the money. For a time, this overshadowed other possibilities.

There came a point when June's unemployment benefits were running out and we focused on generating "Now Money" -- earning enough to provide necessary living expenses on a temporary basis. This was living in Current Reality and facing facts. She indeed took some part-time work to meet her current expenses, which allowed her to keep up her job search. During this process many fascinating discoveries were made and new opportunities came up.

I knew her real needs were more than financial, as is true with every one of my clients. Once she began to earn some income, we began to look at the reality of what she could do that would be genuinely satisfying to her. We must assess, I suggested, these intangible factors as vital to her work and prosperity as well. June took a direction away from looking for a job with a large company. It was revealed in consecutive sessions that June really loved to instruct, teach, and supervise. Hands-on programming and analyzing were things she could do, but these skills did not hold her interest nearly as much as teaching them to others. Focusing on this, she attracted a few private pupils. A part-time job as a computer instructor at a local college gave her more income still.

Work begets work and a positive disposition attracts abundance and the cash was beginning to flow in. June heard of a small company that needed help in making presentations of computer systems to their clients. With her experience and credibility as an instructor at a local college, she was immediately hired. She became so valued at that company that she negotiated two raises in less than eight months, finally making nearly $1,400 a week. This plus her teaching income is now earning her an average of more than $75,000 annually ($10,000 more than her last job). There are ideas being discussed to teach and train others on a larger scale in the future. In addition, her attorney, whom she can now afford to pay, says there is a good chance of gaining custody of her child.

June is feeling extremely capable and confident. She wants to make even more money so she can buy a home and provide an abundant lifestyle for both herself and her child. Though she still has some challenges in debts to repay, dealing with the child custody process and finding even more satisfying work outlets, she has made tremendous strides. Her approaches and attitudes to work and life have shifted, and she lives for more than just a paycheck -- as she had before. She is working toward a number of visions that previously seemed impossible to reach.

June's remarkable reversal took time and was not without discomfort and hardship. It happened through her courage and persistence and by focusing her energies in a new direction while staying in Current Reality. June's triumphs came from bearing discomfort and continuing to adjust, as appropriate, the actions she took with new attitudes behind them. She learned she did not need to act urgently and could live in the present as well as plan ahead. She did this based on the day to day facts of her situation.

REMINDERS:

- **If you are willing to face your Current Reality, you will gain a strong desire to improve your situation.**

- **You do not have to deny your circumstances or force solutions to fix them.**

- **You can be willing to take a look at your financial situation without taking action.**

- **Go slowly in looking at your situation and separate feelings from facts.**

- If your financial situation calls for concern, you can address it as a concern -- not an emergency.

- You can take actions by getting positive support and working calmly on solutions.

- You have the right to get help with your money problems.

- You can change the facts of your circumstances by consistent, <u>not instant</u>, efforts.

MAKE WHAT YOU WANT IMPORTANT

CHAPTER 12

> *When a man decides to take a journey,*
> *the world steps aside to let him pass.*
> adapted from a Buddhist saying

By the time I began this chapter, I found my motivation for writing and finishing the first draft of this book wavering. I sincerely wanted to complete the first draft, revise it, and finish the project, but I simply did not feel as motivated to keep going. My pace had slowed down. I found myself writing less each day. Recurring thoughts of "Get it over with already," kept cropping up. It seemed to take much more effort to sit at my computer keyboard and keep going. I was experiencing emotional resistance and even physical discomfort. Certainly, I am not the first person to have had these experiences writing, but that thought did not seem to help me in this very solitary task. There was something in me, as happens with many of us, that wanted to set my goal aside and pick it up at some point in the future.

This was resistance in the form of procrastination and self-sabotage. In this state, I, like so many others, easily forgot or dismissed the bright promise of the original decision to pursue my goal. The original positive energy that served as my initial inspiration was giving way to thoughts and feelings of frustration and ambivalence. In similar situations in the past, I had been quite adept at rationalizing my "down" mood and would give up on ideas and plans that seemed initially exciting. As continuing seemed more difficult, the old thoughts like "Just stop for a couple of weeks until I feel like doing this again. Do I really want to do this? Maybe I was mistaken. If it's this hard maybe it's best if I try something else," were very strong and convincing. However, after much experience with my own circumstances and those of my clients, I knew to stop abruptly would be self-depriving though continuing would take much emotional effort, temporarily. Fortunately, I had learned from these experiences to keep going, no matter how slowly or falteringly I went on. The key was in making the writing of this book very important to me.

DISMISSING OUR DESIRES

Children naturally seek the approval of their parents, guardians, and teachers. Ideally, our primary caretakers validate us and tell us we are okay in the world. We come to these people with many, many needs. The task of caring for children is a serious and often overwhelming responsibility. Unfortunately, it is not uncommon to have many of our wants and needs ignored, neglected and criticized. After all, our parents were so busy trying to contend with life. Many of us grew up in environments where we mistakenly came to believe our wants and needs were bad. To be acceptable to our parents or others, we learned to hide these wants and needs, abandon them, dismiss them, and criticize them as undesirable and unreasonable. Some of us may even have been punished for expressing our independent needs and desires. These needs got many of us into trouble and were the cause of much frustration in our parents or guardians -- at least that is how we came to view them. It is no surprise why we often deny ourselves and go along with the wishes of others. We learned to do this to be accepted and loved and/or avoid the anger and rejection of our primary caretakers. In other words, we dismissed our desires in order to survive.

Far too many of us have carried this self-denial into adulthood. Many of us become experts at twisting our real needs out of shape to conform with what we believe is acceptable to others. The odd thing is: while we dismiss our desires trying to please someone else, they can, in turn, dismiss their desires trying to please someone besides you. A vicious cycle of self-denial can ensue. For example, a spouse who wants to spend more time with his mate may be in pain about it. He tries to understand his partner's busy schedule, but it distresses and upsets him. His partner, in turn, is not as available because she is breaking her neck at work trying to please a boss who, in turn, is frightened he will lose a demanding client if highly pressured and unreasonable deadlines are not met. The chain of self-deprivation becomes a forged and solidified cycle of people pleasing.

If you are not familiar with this term, one practical definition of people pleasing is: abandoning your own reasonable wants and needs, for the wants, needs and demands of someone else (who is probably busy taking care of themselves or someone else besides you). The interesting thing is we can do this when we are all by ourselves. We do not need anyone around to abandon ourselves and dismiss our desires. At home alone, we can put off something we might like to do because, even in our thinking, we know someone else would disapprove or we think what we want is not as important as what we "should" be doing.

Many of us have learned to focus so heavily on the approval and desires of others that we may not even understand what we need. Others of us never learned that our desires were worthy and deserved to be taken seriously. We received direct and indirect messages that our needs and wants were not really important. Then, it became easy to abandon any ideas or efforts when we felt challenged. We may or may not make a conscious effort to please others, but we certainly have learned to view our genuine goals and dreams (those that motivate and please ourselves) with skepticism because we can "get by" without them (they are not that important anyway). In the end it does not matter what desires and needs we pursue; it only matters that we try to persistently make an effort toward our *perceived* wants.

No matter what it may be, we can assume you have some need or want that you have not followed. Or, if you have acted upon a goal unsuccessfully, you may be contemplating giving it up. In either case, do not to give up on your wants, needs, and dreams. Make them important.

MAKING A DECISION

Before taking any practical steps, we need to act in support of our desires. Our needs and wants must become vital and important. This is accomplished by an action of the mind. We must make the internal decision that *what we want is important*. We must decide that our desires are important enough to initiate, important enough to pursue and important enough to attain.

The challenge and the opportunity here is that you are the only person who can make this decision. If anyone other than yourself decides what desires are important to you, you have defeated the purpose of becoming self-led, confident, and internally prosperous. What is important to you is not a small matter, no matter how "small" the matter is.

A decision is an action of the mind and spirit. In making what we want important, we recondition our minds and spirits to care for our own opinions more than the opinions of others. Yes, we want support from others, but support usually comes once we decide to proceed on our own behalf and continue to do so.

The struggle we face is not with someone's approval or disapproval any longer. Unless we are psychologically unstable, our actual survival does not depend upon anyone's approval as it did when we were children. It is the struggle within us to approve of ourselves, we must face.

We, in fact, may find that others will disapprove of our choices. Yet, only by deciding to make what we want important can we summon up the necessary tools and stamina to meet natural human disapproval, doubt, disappointment, and other obstacles. It is in making what we want *vital* (and this means really vital) that builds our internal fortitude which allows us to make mistakes and continue until we triumph or change our goals. This fortitude allows us to care for ourselves differently, perhaps in a much greater way, than our guardians and caretakers ever did.

Making a decision that your desires are important does not mean that every one of them will be met. It means that you are willing to view your desires as acceptable, reasonable, and obtainable by self-led efforts.

Fear of Loss

One way we sabotage our efforts in pursuing our goals is by operating on the fear of loss. The threat of loss can be real. If you decide your desire to go back to work is important to you, and you follow it, your spouse or mate may not tolerate your unavailability. While it may be important to break a date with a friend to work on something important to you, when you normally would just put it aside, the friend may be hurt and angry and not make any more plans with you. Loss happens in real life. All of us must learn to withstand the fear of it, however.

Loss can occur in many ways. By beginning to do what is really important to you, there may be conflict with those who are comfortable with the way you *were* operating. You can lose a sense of comfort in your professional and personal relationships. If others learn to accept your new behavior, however, you will likely have even stronger and healthier relationships with them. In pursuing your needs and wants, you may also need to let go of some things you do not now have time for. What we have spent time on has created an image of who we are (or, should it be who we have wanted others to think we are?). You may lose the benefits of living up to this image. Your genuine desires may become obvious and open to judgment. That is fine, if you have internally judged what you are doing as good and right for you and you are prepared to get support to help you keep going.

If you stop doing some things and pursue what you really want, others will begin to see a new you by the new choices you are making. Your efforts will become visible and apparent to others. You will, however, be putting yourself on the line for real and right reasons, not just to uphold an image of yourself that you believe is acceptable. By making a decision that what you want is important, you will also give yourself the motivation to create a plan of action or inspire your resourcefulness to explore your goal and attain it. In doing this, and pursuing your desires with clear intent, you will make choices. Other things you are currently doing will likely need to be set aside or fall by the wayside. This is not a problem. It is actually a wonderful by-product of making decisions. Eventually you will learn to do mostly those things that stimulate and please you. However, initially this may go against your training as you try to keep everything in place *and* you pursue your desires. After a while, you will learn to let go of trying to do those things that really do not require your attention.

Loss understandably feels threatening. Therefore, it is suggested to start slowly. Right now, as best you can, begin to make a decision that some of your "smaller" desires such as reading a favorite book or magazine are important. Go to a restaurant you really enjoy and do not compromise for the sake of companionship that day. Work up to telling your boss you cannot work late on the nights you do not want to work late. Tell a relative that you do not have time to talk because you need to do something else.

If we are willing to define ourselves through our desires and our pursuits, we will lose some things and gain others. Change does involve loss. We may lose a sense of belonging in the form of familiar activities and people. There is a also sense of security in acting and behaving the way we have always acted and behaved. When we begin to do things differently, according to our true needs, we may lose the sense of safety (familiarity) we had. As we make decisions based on what we genuinely want, we stop falsely portraying ourselves to others for their approval. This is apt to change some of our relationships (loss of the old form of the relationship). In being true to ourselves, there may be fear in us and confusion or anger in others. These reactions can combine to temporarily give us an overall sense of anxiety and loss. Even if this occurs, there is so much we can gain. As we learn to do what is important for us, and grow by the experiences of doing so, we will fortify ourselves internally. This will help us accept ourselves as we are and find more value in following our true nature and in expressing ourselves authentically. As we acquire the knowledge and skills to live honestly, we will want to fulfill our genuine needs, do things that satisfy us and attract others who support us and our true desires.

Yet, facing the fear of loss is difficult, especially when it is possible loss will occur. It can be done, however, if you are willing to experience *the feelings* that come with following your desires and deciding to make them important. For most of us, withstanding the possibility of loss and acting on our own behalf, despite fears and other obstacles, is an essential part of allowing more abundance into our lives. Making what you want important and risking loss may be going against deeply ingrained beliefs that have been stopping you for years. It is vital to remember, once again, to proceed slowly if intense emotional triggers arise. To make progress in pursuing what you want, you do not need to put yourself in extreme risk or jeopardy. With patient practice and time, the fear of loss and actual loss will not keep you from moving toward greater satisfaction and prosperity in your life.

DEMONSTRATING YOUR SERIOUSNESS

As mentioned repeatedly in previous chapters, you do not have to take any action in order to simply *consider* these ideas. All you need to do is think them through -- ruminate about them. Yet, if we are to take raising our level of prosperity seriously, it is at this point we must discuss action. If you are still reading this book for its ideas, that is fine. Come back, however, to this point because action is the vehicle through which prosperous principles find expression.

In reading this chapter, several desires have probably come to your mind that you may have previously neglected or dismissed. Pick one or two of these desires that are not particularly threatening or will not set off an intense fear of loss if you act upon them. If you are to stop depriving yourself and live more abundantly, you must demonstrate your seriousness through action. You are not responsible for the results, only your efforts. Your determination to act upon new principles means that you, by necessity, are making what you want important.

Any action is great. It does not matter if it works. The only requirement is that it has the possibility of moving you ahead. In other words, taking action is not an exercise in empty gestures. Actions need to be sincere and serious attempts to get what you want. If the issue you face is too large, take small actions. For example, if you want to go back to college, and that seems scary, simply call up different schools and have them mail course catalogues to you. If you want to make more money at your job, figure out how much of a raise you want and write it down.

Of course, one action alone seldom accomplishes a goal or fully displays our seriousness. If we are to have what we want, we need to make it important and keep showing our serious intent through *persistent action*. It is only through many applications of a different philosophy that gives a principle the chance to work. This makes common sense. We do not lose weight exercising one or two days and stopping. We do not buy a house by saving money for three months and quitting. It is not unusual though, that we want to have the ends without going through the means. We have learned, in this age, to be creatures of convenience and comfort. In far too many instances, we are afraid to demonstrate serious intent and work patiently toward our goals. The paradox is: if we are willing to do the work, the work eventually becomes easier to do. We gain strength by exercising new emotional muscles -- bearing the discomfort of pursuing what we now view as important.

PRAISE EFFORTS, NOT RESULTS

Endorse and praise yourself for your efforts, not the results they bring. Taking action, then, becomes the goal in and of itself. As you move ahead, constantly tell yourself how great it is that you are willing to consider new philosophies and take new actions, no matter how imperfectly you move along.

It is only natural to want our actions to turn out a specific way. We always hope that a minimum of effort will be needed to accomplish our goals. However, in taking action we can make mistakes, hit dead ends, or find we are not getting anywhere with some of our efforts. This is natural, even healthy and desirable. It is through this learning process that we find what works for us. If our focus is on specific, expected results, it is easy to become discouraged and disappointed. We can lose respect for ourselves if, by focusing on outcomes, we cannot force specific results in a specific time frame. We can then give up our desires easily or procrastinate until all of our previous efforts lose their impact. Also, by expecting a specific conclusion to our endeavors, we can lose sight of other opportunities that may turn out better than our original plans.

We must practice focusing on efforts. All efforts made with a genuine desire to help ourselves and grow in our personal and professional endeavors are noble and admirable. Get support from others who believe this philosophy. We live in a results-oriented society, so that is often not easy. We are constantly measured by external and unrealistic criteria. This robs us of our humanity and sets most of us up for failure. If we succeed in attaining the "approval" of society in our accomplishments, we can become slaves to the judgments of our "masters."

For example, I hope this book reaches many people and is useful to them. There would be much personal benefit in this. There are certain results that would be exciting if they occurred. However, it is exceedingly clear it is far more important that this book is written and completed, no matter what the outcome. In doing so, there are benefits gained simply by making this decision important, applying principles of prosperity as the writing proceeds, and allowing growth and learning from the experience. Then all the efforts made will be in line with becoming more prosperous, and regardless of the outcome, the process will provide strength on the road toward greater fulfillment and abundance.

We show ourselves and the world our character through our efforts and intent. As we develop courage and stamina by defining our wants and needs and pursuing them persistently, we change inside. It is this inner change that is truly important, regardless of the results of our efforts. This is what attracts greater prosperity and adds to the quality of our lives. We often face the choice of the more familiar way or the way that eventually strengthens our spirit and makes self-care and abundant living second nature.

It's Never Too Late to Pursue Something Important

Barbara was 59 and a semi-retired demographics/polling expert living in Minneapolis. Over the years she had owned a company and raised a family. She managed to save and invest a comfortable sum of money, some of which came from selling her share of the business to her partner. One thing that prompted her departure was the terminal illness of her husband. Upon his passing, Barbara decided to stop working for a while. Eventually, Barbara rented a small office so that she could pursue a part-time business as an independent consultant to polling companies around the country. The difficulty of her personal loss eased over time, yet Barbara found it quite difficult to acquire clients despite her excellent reputation in the field. Confused and uncertain about her next move, she contacted me to help her organize her business papers and files. She believed it would help her make more effective decisions about what materials to send out to promote her services as a consultant.

Barbara thought her main obstacle was that she was disorganized. Indeed, she was, but the paper jungle she created in her office environment was really just a tangible indication that she had lost her sense of direction. It is very common to have a messy office when one is confused and without direction.

It was understandable and clear that her husband's death had shaken her foundation. At first, my job was to help her get grounded again, not to help her with a filing system as she originally believed. Instead, we directed her energies toward getting some consulting clients. It took several months, but at last she landed a client who hired her to oversee some polling projects. After completing a few of these projects, Barbara felt confident and capable again. Earning money again with her talents invigorated her.

When we discussed how many projects she wanted to take on in a year, our talks took another turn. It seemed Barbara had a secret desire she had never really let herself explore. She confided to me that she had always wanted to do something "important" with her research and analytical talents. The projects she typically worked on were for consumer products, such as cars, appliances, and food items. Barbara wondered if she could use her skills to research pressing social and economic issues and offer analysis of them and possible solutions to non-partisan political organizations. When asked what she wanted to work on, she made it clear she was tremendously interested in making a contribution to battling the nation's drug crisis.

I encouraged her to think about this desire and kept asking her, "Why not? Why not you? Why can't you research and write about this as well as anyone? If you make this important to you, you will find a way to do it." She eventually took this statement to heart and began to explore ways to follow her desire. Over the course of the next year and a half, Barbara went about researching the drug problem using her many years of professional experience. She made this very important. So important, in fact, she let go of trying to get other consulting clients. This work vitalized and energized her. She became devoted to this task and researched and wrote for two years on the subject. Now, Barbara is soliciting the help of a professional editor to help her formulate articles and possibly a book on the subject. This is the type of work Barbara had always dreamed of. She had always longed to make a difference in her community.

It would seem as though Barbara had the luxury of not having to earn an income to pursue her dreams. To a degree, it is true that she was able to rely on her savings for a time. On the other hand, she was actually running her own research project and incurring business expenses without any certainty her efforts would generate any revenue. For her, money was steadily going out and income was not coming in. Like any of us who want to pursue what is important to us, we need to invest our time and often money, without the guarantee that our efforts will manifest in the results we hope for. We would all need to do this, as Barbara did, while attending to other aspects of our lives. Though difficult for her, Barbara decided to take this risk and make an investment in herself and her dreams.

Whether Barbara's work gets published, meets with approval, is helpful to civic and health organizations, or simply becomes a personal journey of discovery, she made it important to herself. This enabled her to find a direction that was stimulating, challenging and more fulfilling. Regardless of her "success" in the world with this direction, she will keep learning and growing. With encouragement, she took a desire, made it important, and demonstrated her intent by following through. She elevated her sense of self-esteem and inner strength. In making what she wanted important and acting upon it, Barbara changed internally. In doing this, she began taking better care of her physical health, made better financial decisions, and worked to improve her relationships with her adult children.

Wherever her endeavors take her, she has gained a great deal from the principle of seriously pursuing her desires. It was not her destination that made the difference; it was listening to her true needs, making them important and pursuing them, despite obstacles and uncertainly. This is what changed Barbara, gave her a renewed sense of purpose, and improved the way she lives and interacts in the world.

REMINDERS:

- You can make a decision that what you want is important.

- You no longer need to dismiss your desires.

- You can begin to take actions to demonstrate that you take your needs seriously.

- In moving toward more abundance, you can overcome the loss of familiar and "comfortable" aspects of your life.

- What you will gain in prosperity and well-being is worth facing the fear of losing some of what you have now.

- Praise and endorse yourself continuously for your efforts, regardless of the results.

- You can be what you were intended to be and go where you were intended to go.

- You can learn to be truthful with yourself and faithful to your goals.

FOLLOW ABUNDANCE

CHAPTER 13

Sometimes you polish it here and it shines over there.
A not-so-common wise saying

In the previous chapter, we explored the issues of making what we want important, demonstrating our seriousness through action, and endorsing ourselves for our efforts, not the results. However, even though we need to pursue what we *think* we want, there is no certainty that we will land where we are heading. If we are to enjoy greater prosperity, we must diligently follow our desires but allow the results to unfold before us and show us where to proceed. This is the paradox embodied in the principle of committing to your desires yet letting go of what you want.

This does not mean that we abandon our goals. It simply means that if good fortune presents itself elsewhere, go with it. In this regard, we must be willing to let go of our ideas of what we want when abundance is pointing us elsewhere. It is terrific when our efforts end in results that go exactly according to plan. However, it can be just as satisfying, maybe even surprising and wonderful, when our efforts take us elsewhere. Besides, we cannot force the world to give us particular outcomes any more than we can force the weather to act on our command or force someone to live the way we think they should. If we take the action and let go of specific and expected results, we can benefit in wonderful ways.

Here is my favorite example of this principle, one that you may be familiar with. It is the story of the invention of the telephone.

The invention of the telephone, by Alexander Graham Bell, came about by surprise -- through an accident. Mr. Bell married a woman who had a deaf child and devoted much of his life to helping people who were hearing-impaired. In 1871, Alexander Graham Bell moved to Boston and opened a school for teachers of the deaf. During this time he worked on many devices to aid the sufferers of serious hearing loss -- including instruments to help them learn to communicate. At one point, he began to work on a particular device to help the deaf learn to speak. Bell came to the conclusion that he did not have the time nor expertise to succeed with this project by himself. He hired Thomas A. Watson, a local man experienced with electrical instruments. In early June 1875, while both men were working on this device, Bell heard sounds emanating from an instrument in his room that came via a connection to an instrument in another room where Watson was working. What Bell heard on his instrument were sounds coming from reeds (similar to the kind used in musical instruments) that were attached to an electrical device in Watson's room. Bell beckoned to Watson, "Stop what you are doing. Don't change a thing." Not knowing what had happened, they experimented with these reed sounds and transmitted them from one instrument to the other for about one hour. The very next day, during the course of further experimentation and adjustment to the device, Bell spilled acid and uttered the fateful phrase, "Watson, come in here. I need you." Watson now heard audible voice sounds coming from his instrument. Unexpectedly, the first telephone call had been made. After several months of refinement, Bell was issued a patent for this incredible invention on March 7, 1876. (Mr. Watson shared in the abundance that followed when Mr. Bell gave him a share of the invention's profits.)

The device Bell constructed was not meant to do what it did. Mr. Bell had a serious intent to help the deaf. In his wildest dreams, he probably never conceived of the future results of his original goal. Isn't it now ironic the deaf can communicate with one another throughout the world over telephone lines and satellites which evolved as a totally unpredictable result of Mr. Bell's efforts?! Pardon the pun, but Abundance called him in another direction. We are the benefactors of his unsuccessful original purpose.

We can all find instances in our own lives that have turned out differently than we intended and all for the better. The reason for bringing this subject up is to remind ourselves that we cannot control outcomes; nor do we need to. It is our initial clarity, intention, and purpose that matter. If we remember that our self-worth is more than the attainment of specific goals, we are free to follow results as they unfold. We can operate diligently and freely toward our destination, yet be willing to shift course if that is where opportunity takes us. We do not need to know where we will land. If it is different from what we originally wanted, chances are very good it is a much better place than we intended.

ESSENCE OVER FORM

One excellent way to keep motivated without fixating on results is by keeping your focus on the essential elements or qualities you are trying to attain, rather than all of the specific details of your goals. In other words, be open to accepting the **essence** of what you want. If you wish to live in an apartment building with a doorman, for instance, the essence of what you want may be a sense of security. The **form** you have chosen in your mind is a doorman. If you remain open to having another form, but the same essence, you may find yourself living across the street from a police station or another residence (form) that makes you feel secure. If you have a day job but want to make more money from your home business, the essence of what you want may be to work less and have more flexible hours. The essence of this is more time and more freedom. It may be possible to ask for a raise and negotiate better hours at your regular job. It is a solution that might be worth a try. If you want a bigger living space, the essence might be to enjoy a sense of openness around you. You certainly could move, but it may be possible to sell some things or put them in storage, repaint your home in a light color and even have a big picture window constructed in a place where there is now a wall. Focus on the essence of what you want. Abundance may follow in a different form.

You do not have to give up the essence of what you desire, even if you cannot attain the exact form of it. It is common to want more money and freedom, respect, security, less pressure, more creative endeavors, and better relationships. Stay with these desires. If one form does not give this to you, open your mind to having your overall desires met in another way.

We can logically surmise the essence of what Alexander Graham Bell was aiming for was to help people communicate. Boy did that happen! It did not happen exactly the way he expected, but his profits from the telephone patent enabled him to continue his research and efforts in helping the deaf. Over time, Bell's invention has helped deaf individuals the world over. By being mindful of the qualities and elements of what you want, you can gain remarkable freedom and success. The key is in appreciating and being satisfied by attaining the essence of what you are aiming for. In choosing this perspective, where once you might have seen failure, because you did not reach the specifics of your goals, you can see victory and enjoy the underlying elements of your desires.

We do not need to force our desires and plans on the world. If we do so, we will find life does not often cooperate with us. The price we pay in discouragement and frustration can be quite high. It is a paradox to pursue what we want with serious intent, yet let go of specific results. If we accept this paradox, however, we can end up in circumstances that are more wonderful than we could have even thought.

If we let ourselves go *with* the results as they unfold, amazing things can happen. If our plans go well, we only need open our minds to following the abundance that comes from pursuing what we want.

— ❧ — THEY WENT TOGETHER, THEN TOOK DIFFERENT ROUTES, AND CAME TOGETHER AGAIN IN SPIRIT — ❧ —

Mary and Karen were partners in a business venture. They were trying to break into the greeting card industry. Administration and sales were Mary's primary responsibilities. The creative aspects went to Karen, who was an illustrator and design expert. This pair of intelligent and skilled women matched well in temperament and goals. Mary had put together a wonderful and thorough business plan that they used to find investors for their business. Karen had made some new card designs that were unique and compelling. They were successful in getting several New York stationery stores to buy and sell their cards. However, they were barely covering expenses. The investors' money had just about run out and Mary was living off her rapidly dwindling savings. Karen was earning a decent income in her individual career as an illustrator; yet she was quite frustrated that their joint vision was not taking off. This is when we first met.

—◇◇◇—

Mary and Karen told me they had gone into the business because it seemed fun, creative, and potentially lucrative. Besides, they each liked being with another person who shared so much of the same personal traits and views. These were good reasons to join forces. I pointed out, though, the possibility that the business venture might not work. Yet, I assured them they could still each enjoy greater satisfaction, creativity, and prosperity individually. They had, obviously, considered the idea they might not be successful with their new company but had not really faced this question squarely.

I asked them to commit to being prosperous whether it came from this business venture or came individually. Examining the possibility that the business might not work was not to discourage them. The point was to open their minds to the idea that there are many options and avenues to prosperity. They agreed to consider this but naturally hoped success would come from their combined efforts. With prosperity as their guide post, we worked to create revenue for the struggling greeting card business. Within a few months, it was evident this business was not going to pay salaries for some time. Due to a dwindling financial reserve, Mary needed to begin looking for work. I reminded her it was a wise choice to take care of her current financial needs while working toward her vision. Money for daily living was, of course, crucial. Most of us cannot become abundant when we live on the financial edge or continually feel fearful and poor.

As Mary looked for a job, she and Karen agreed to keep up efforts, as much as possible, in their joint venture. So, we continued to meet to move their business forward. Now, however, Mary and Karen began to see me individually as well. From thereon their stories, as I suspected, took different paths.

Mary

Mary found a job with an investment company helping them develop a financial data base. Her previous work experience opened the door for this opportunity. Initially hired as a temporary employee, it was immediately apparent that Mary's level of service was higher than the level of salary accompanying it. This made her unhappy and resentful. We discussed how this made her feel frustrated, angry and, at times, depressed. Underearning creates pressure which provokes stressful feelings.

With these feelings (inner messages) as her guide, Mary determined that she should get a considerable increase in her pay rate. We outlined a campaign to get a raise. Although Mary's supervisor said he agreed with her in principle, he told her his hands were tied and could not raise her pay rate. We did not let this deter our intent and Mary kept persisting at finding arguments to get a raise. Within a few weeks, the supervisor agreed to change certain procedures that allowed Mary to earn an additional $8 per hour. During the next few months, Mary saw an opportunity to create a permanent position for herself at the investment company. She feared it might take her even further away from the joint venture with Karen but she knew she wanted to live more abundantly. I encouraged her to move ahead with her plan. After three months of assertive action, Mary became an junior officer of the company at a salary close to $50,000 annually. This rejuvenated her confidence that had eroded during the struggles with the joint business venture. Having stabilized her income, the time had come to address the delayed joint venture in some way.

After some probing, we discovered one of Mary's prime motivations in teaming with Karen. Mary had a creative side and wanted to be in a "creative" business. With her financial background, she never considered using her creative talents directly. She had thought, in teaming with an artist, she could be around creativity in her career. I pointed out it was possible to for her to pursue her own artistic interests directly. Living vicariously off the work of others, including her dear friend Karen, diminished her chances for genuine satisfaction. We talked about how she could include creativity directly into her life.

After a short while, Mary began taking writing classes. Giving herself this gratification was a completely new experience. Operating under the principle of following abundance, Mary and I sometimes allude in our discussions to professional writing. It remains open as to whether professional writing is in her future. Why not? People write for a living. This possibility is just as likely as a less creative scenario. Mary is now exploring more fully how she will use her creativity directly to provide an income. She recently has shown her work in professional circles. It became clear that Mary and Karen's business venture was an attempt to accomplish together what they needed to do apart; that is, find their own path of abundance.

Karen

When Karen started to work with me individually, we talked about two of her most persistent obstacles. The issues were: the high number of hours she worked and the low rates she charged. She was making a decent living, but too often worked long days and weekends in her illustration and graphic design career. I suggested the possibility of working less and making more money. Finding this intriguing, she was willing to talk further, though she wasn't totally convinced it could work for her. However, she showed a willingness to try my suggestions. With consistent effort, Karen raised her rates and made more money in less time. Eventually she began to drop the lower-paying clients. In the next six months she cut her hours down by almost a third and increased her income more than 20%. Not so unexpectedly, as her prices increased, her creative ideas were even more respected by her clients. During the first six months of the next calendar year, she generated more than $60,000. This amount was more than her total income from the entire year before. Karen had clearly assimilated the idea of being more financially abundant.

Feeling more confident, she allowed herself to travel in more prestigious circles and began to meet advertising agency executives. In July, after her best six months ever, Karen landed her first national advertising campaign. She garnered $20,000 net profit for approximately four weeks of work. The illustration in this campaign, which the advertisers loved, was Karen's vision. The clients were interested in using the style she created for the next year or more, and she recently completed another campaign with them for a handsome sum. By the year's end, she grossed more than $100,000 -- doubling her income from her best year ever. During this time, Karen began saving money and gave herself new equipment, new clothes, vacations, took her weekends off, and generally elevated her lifestyle. She began to do new things and meet new people. One man she met spent considerable time with her and shared her vision of the future and they are soon to be married. Quite successfully, Karen learned to earn and give herself more income in less time, enjoy more creative freedom and follow the process as it was unfolding. As she followed abundance, things happened in her professional and personal life that were unexpected and wonderful.

—◇◇◇—

Both Mary and Karen are thriving independently and remain good friends. They are paying off their investors from their business venture *while enjoying much more independent, prosperous lifestyles. Of equal importance is the sense of satisfaction each of them experiences. In supporting and following their own creative energies, they went to different and more abundant places than they originally planned.*

REMINDERS:

- Pursue your wants and needs, but open your mind to new possibilities, directions, goals, and destinations.

- Follow abundance. Go where it leads you.

- You do not need to control the outcome of your efforts.

- You can let results take you to a better place than you originally planned.

- Keep your mind open to achieving your goals in other forms.

- By accepting the essence of what you want, you have found success.

Act on the Assumption
That Success Is Possible

CHAPTER 14

*All things are possible until they are proved impossible --
and even the impossible may only be so, as of now.*
Pearl S. Buck

If we operate under the belief that progress is extremely difficult, it is because we experience it that way. We may get to the point where every goal we want to attain seems fraught with obstacles. It may seem as though we need to greatly exert ourselves with no certainty that our efforts will work. In so thinking, many of us discourage ourselves even before we begin to act. We fall into the trap of viewing ourselves and our abilities as insufficient to achieve our desires. If this is so, we come to view the challenges before us as enormous. At times we do not know what we can do to make progress. This can keep us in a state of inaction that seems insurmountable. In past experiences, we may have tried diligently to meet responsibilities or pursue goals and fell short of our mark. This too can leave us with the sense that we are incapable of meeting more than our basic needs, and perhaps not even those.

Even though these feelings are not factual and represent a negative interpretation of events, it would be rare to find a person who did not at some time experience a sense of immobilization, inadequacy, and humiliation. Our perceived failures take a toll on our self-esteem, and, in this state, we are much less likely to move out into the world. This is a very common human experience.

Becoming blocked and unmotivated is such a common occurrence that a whole industry focusing on motivation has arisen. One could even say this book would generally fall into that category. The point is, we all experience setbacks from which we need to recover.

We can assume, in some aspect of your life, prior negative experiences and fears are holding you back. One very effective way to counteract this problem is to act on the assumption that you could *possibly* succeed in your efforts. Acting on this assumption can overcome emotional blocks, motivate you, and renew the sense that you are capable. This means you acknowledge it is a possibility, not a certainty, that taking action *could* yield positive results.

As an example, you decide to mail a resume for a job on the possibility, *no matter how slight you may think it is,* that you could get an interview. You act *despite the thought* "the odds are against me." With this action, you acted on the assumption that securing an interview is in the realm of possibility. As another example, you are at a social event and you see a striking-looking person. You approach this individual and say hello on the simple, logical possibility they *might* be available and find you interesting. *Even if you are feeling insecure about yourself,* it is possible you can hit it off with them.

When you act on the assumption that success is possible, you are not invalidating the chance (even at times, the likelihood) your efforts will not work out. On the contrary, you are fully aware that any individual action or plan may not yield positive results. You have simply accepted the premise it is in the realm of possibility that your action or plan has a *chance* of working.

We may need to unblock and motivate ourselves on a small scale at first. Acting on the assumption that success is possible is like building a muscle. You start with actions with which you can bear the discomfort of a negative response or non-response. For example, you telephone a friend to ask them to join you at the movies at the last minute. They may say no, or not even be home to take your call. This is a negative or non-response most of us can easily survive. As you continue to take these kinds of small actions, you will strengthen your ability to withstand disappointment with less threatening goals, which then paves the way for *possible* triumph with more significant desires. (There will also be positive results as well as you experiment with this.) As you overcome the resistance you have to experiencing negative or non-responses, you may find it becomes progressively easier to take actions.

If you feel blocked and unmotivated to take new action, ask yourself if what you want is possible in the real world -- *for someone*. Is someone doing what you want to do, or does someone have what you want to have? If it is possible in the real world for someone, then it is possible (though not certain) for you.

You do not need to believe your actions will work; you only need to be willing to act on the possibility that good things can happen to you. If they do not, that is fine. All of us have experienced things not working out. We have survived negative results and we can do so again. This is not to deny you might feel bad if your attempts do not work. Indeed, you may feel the sting of trying unsuccessfully to move ahead. However, if you act on possibilities and are willing to withstand these experiences and try again, you can motivate and unblock yourself with great effect.

If what you want is realistic (meaning doable by others of similar skills and talents), there is an absolute possibility you can accomplish your realistic dreams as well. You do not have to believe this is true. You simply need to intellectually agree, that if others of similar talents and abilities can do well, it is possible *you* can succeed in your attempts to grow.

If you do not believe you deserve to have what you want, that is fine also. Again, you do not have to believe anything. You only need to attempt to act upon your goals. If you attain a goal you think you do not deserve, you can always get rid of your triumph or cease to support it and it will disappear. That is your choice. Let us not, however, deny the possibility we can succeed in our endeavors.

Even if your efforts have failed in the past, it is possible new actions taken with a new perspective could work with former goals. If you need to get support, go to a caring friend or colleague and talk with them about your plans. Then, take an action and contact your friend again after its completion to discuss the experience.

Remember these vital points from prior chapters: *Actions are results in and of themselves. We take actions on the possibility they might work, but they need not work to positively affect us.*

If you still feel too frightened, or are delaying taking action, then you may be picking an action that is too large and important to you. If you are having trouble, break goals down into the smallest possible steps. For instance, if you want to ask for a raise, figure out exactly how much more money you would like. Begin talking to others who have asked for raises and have successfully received them. Then, find out if your company offers raises to its employees beyond normal yearly increases. Ask your supervisor if they have ever given anyone a raise. Tell your supervisor you would like to talk about a raise for yourself, without asking for one. Meet with your supervisor about the actual raise. Still do not ask; use this time to discuss the merits of your work and your financial needs. Leave this discussion open-ended. Come back and specifically ask for the raise. Each step needs to be taken separately and over time. This process could take weeks. It may work; it may not. It does not matter, in the sense that you are only asking. If you can withstand a No answer, then you can slowly move ahead. You can gain inner fortitude whatever the outcome. Many of my clients have made noble attempts which have not worked, yet felt stronger and a had greater sense of self-respect for having tried to reach a goal.

Use Outside Assistance

Get help if you are struggling by yourself. Do not stay alone with your frustration. Remember, it is prosperous to ask for help. If you cannot seem to take action or make the smallest of steps, you may need professional counseling or coaching to enable you to move ahead and discuss the outcomes of your actions. Others can help you operate with the right attitudes and survive disappointments. This will fortify your future efforts and help you to make progress and prosperity a reality.

Acting As If

You could operate your whole life based on the idea that you may not succeed but were willing to act on the possibility you could. In years past, I distinctly remember a number of times that I said to myself in a painful negative mantra, "This won't work. This won't work. This won't work. This won't work." I tried certain actions anyway and many actions did not work - *but inevitably some did.* The process helped me break the belief that nothing I did would work. Now, some of my actions always work out as planned or better than I anticipated.

Acting on the assumption that success is possible can free us from years of holding ourselves back. Operating on this principle can release the ghosts of projected fears and negative beliefs.

—◆◆— Never Too Far Down To Try —◆◆—

During our first phone conversation, Alicia informed me that she was suffering from a clinical depression. Fired from a job as a corporate executive three years earlier, at the age of 42, she had not worked since. Losing this job triggered a battery of long-hidden emotional scars which finally took their toll. Alicia had given up. To some degree, this makes sense. Our internal wisdom says, "Why continue the strain and uselessness of this way of life?" For some of us, our self-destructive ways of conducting our life comes to a halt and we "hit bottom." We are faced with the prospect of changing or continuing to suffer. Though painful and often frightening, this kind of shock in our circumstances can provide us with necessary motivation to address issues differently. In that regard, Alicia sought professional help for her problems, and a psychiatrist put her on antidepressant medication. Her emotional state was so severe she was receiving disability payments for her clinical depression. This did not dissuade me from attempting to help her. Though she was less than enthusiastic, and lived out of town in Connecticut, Alicia agreed to come to New York and meet me once to see what I could offer her.

—◇◇◇—

I am not a professional therapist, but through painful experiences of my own, I had come to study and understand much about human psychology. I did not want to replace Alicia's therapist; I wanted to find out if Alicia was putting into practice the insights she was gaining in her counseling sessions. She was having trouble doing so. To get Alicia moving in a positive direction again, we examined the "principle of possibility," This means I asked Alicia to concede it was possible for her to improve her situation and her outlook even if she did not know how to do so. When she finally agreed <u>in principle</u> that positive change was possible, though not inevitable, she agreed to keep working with me.

At first I wanted her to see me in person, though her commute took some effort. I knew that to get Alicia moving again, she needed some strong one-on-one support. Our initial work together was focused on getting Alicia into action despite the intense negative feelings and negative interpretations of herself that were immobilizing her. We talked about the kinds of things she did in her weekly routine. It seems that she spent a fair amount of time helping at church services. She also had an interest in the rights of physically disabled persons and often contacted local leaders and politicians urging them to do more for these individuals. Knowing that small steps were called for, I asked Alicia if it was possible to get more involved in the church. After some hedging, she agreed it was possible and she began to participate more in church activities involving the rights of the disabled.

As it happened, a bill requiring companies to make better access for disabled people was coming up for a vote in the state legislature. With Alicia's stepped up involvement in the church's efforts for disabled people, she wanted to participate in supporting the bill. After fully discussing the idea that her efforts did not have to work out, I encouraged her to take even more actions. Since taking actions were viewed as successes in and of themselves, she did not need to focus on the eventual outcome of her efforts. This gave her the perspective she needed to become more involved in passing this bill. As she took actions, some of them produced very positive results from organizations and groups in favor of passing the bill. These responses further supported her and gave her the feeling she was making a genuine contribution. Ultimately, she wrote letters and personally spoke to a half dozen state representatives, including the Speaker of the House. A major feat for someone who did not want to even clean the house just a few months earlier. The bill passed. Knowing her efforts were worthwhile and helpful, Alicia felt more capable than she had in years.

With this experience under her belt, she became willing to face the challenge of earning income again. Even though Alicia was moving again, much fear and anxiety resulted. She did not want to go through the same pressures she had suffered before in her corporate job. Little by little, we talked through all of her concerns and came up with small, doable actions intended to find part-time employment.

Alicia contacted a number of individuals and slowly began to tell others she was available for work. Through this process, a professional acquaintance asked Alicia if she was willing to work as an administrative aide to the president of a brokerage company on an "as needed" basis -- paid by the day. We discussed her options thoroughly, including saying NO for any days she felt she could not work.

The most important thing I asked Alicia was, "Is it possible you can work one day and see how it feels and how it works for you?" She was unsure but agreed it was _possible_ to make it through the day just fine. I assured her that she only had to try it for one day and could stop if she did not want to continue. With much trepidation, she tried it. As you might guess, this worked. Acting on the assumption that she could successfully earn income again, Alicia overcame her projected anxieties and fears. The anticipation that there would be a negative experience was much worse than the real thing. She made it through the day with little negative emotional effect. We both viewed this as a great triumph and tremendous encouragement for the future.

Once believing she would never be able to handle work-related stress again, Alicia has made more than ten thousand dollars in the last few months. She has become a valuable member of the corporate team and has even made numerous solo appearances outside of the office in formal meetings on behalf of the company. Despite battling uncomfortable feelings and negative views of herself, she takes action and continues to slowly build her self-esteem. The depression that paralyzed her has lifted a great deal. Since she is now self-motivated, she does not need to see me in person any longer and we work together over the telephone to great effect. Alicia went from being a person who felt extremely immobilized to an active and much more confident individual. She has challenges in working and balancing life, as we all do, and meets them with courage and a determination to do the best thing for herself. There is every indication she will find meaningful work and continue to act on the growing knowledge that she is a capable and valuable human being. There has been a marked change in her general perspective. Alicia has made great headway on a different journey.

It was not that Alicia's therapy was not helpful. It was incomplete. Coming to intellectual (cognitive) awareness without being guided through significant new experiences will rarely yield any lasting improvements. We need to internally assimilate new experiences, conducted with new philosophies (attitudes). In other words, understanding our difficulties is not enough. Making changes involves taking new actions with new attitudes. Only repetitive attempts at doing things differently, taken despite intense feelings, can give us the internal knowledge and security that we are capable, valuable and are able to withstand negative experiences. These new behaviors need to be repeated over time until we have made them a part of "what we normally do." We can eventually find our inner beliefs changing in a very positive direction. As we learn to act on the assumption that success is possible (and withstand the discomfort of doing so), we give *ourselves the positive reinforcement that we are able to move ahead and enjoy greater success despite our imperfections.*

Some people suffer from disabilities, either physical or mental. Is it possible they can improve their situations? Yes, they can -- without a doubt. If prosperity is a state of consciousness, of internal well-being, then any person willing to change is capable of improving. Alicia is a wonderful example of how this principle works. Her growth was not without fear and discomfort, but there were many triumphs along the way that kept her motivated through bouts with depression. Think of how much potential there is for those of us who do not face extreme emotional or physical challenges. For us, living more abundantly is almost a certainty, if we care to act on the assumption and chance that we will eventually succeed.

REMINDERS:

- Start with smaller goals and acknowledge it is possible for you to reach them.

- You can act as if your efforts might work.

- You can move toward more important goals by taking one action at a time and then pausing until you are ready to take another.

- Make taking actions the result you aim for.

- If we proceed in small steps, we can handle both disappointment and triumph.

- Negative thoughts cannot stop you because you do not need to believe you can succeed to take actions.

- In order to have a positive influence on you, your actions do not need to work.

- As you take new actions with a different perspective, you can eventually come to believe in your own capabilities to a much greater degree.

Give Yourself a Raise

VIEW SETBACKS AS ASSETS

CHAPTER 15

I have failed many times.
Henry Ford, in response to the question,
"To what do you attribute your success?"

No one likes the feeling of having failed. However, it is a simple truth that every endeavor we undertake will not work as planned. We can do everything just right and still not experience a positive outcome. In truth, it is much more likely we will make mistakes and hit dead ends. At times, we will pour our heart, soul, and energy into efforts that fall flat and disintegrate. These experiences are not fun by any means, but they are a necessary part of learning, living, and growing.

In unsuccessful attempts to get what we want and need, it is natural to have the initial reactions of discouragement, frustration, and anger. These setbacks are only a problem, however, if we continue to see them as a mark of our self-worth and self-esteem. Many of us internalize these feelings and hold them as facts about our character. If our efforts do not succeed, we condition ourselves to believe we are not good enough. Whether it is our upbringing that creates this belief or later experiences in life that account for it, we must learn to view our setbacks in a positive light if we are to grow beyond them.

Setbacks are priceless assets. If you already see them as such, you are not the only one who holds this view. Teachers, scientists, and leaders of all kinds herald learning from difficult, even negative experiences, as wholesome, healthy, and desirable. Winning is *not* everything. It is not the *only* thing. In fact, the idea to describe ourselves or anyone as a winner or loser is an absurdity. We all win and we all lose. It's true that some of us have more troubled lives than others or may seemingly have more character flaws than someone else. However, if we have the ability to change, our difficulties can give us invaluable experiences and serve as a catalyst for living differently and abundantly. Yet, if we define ourselves by our perceived successes or failures in comparison to others, we continue to live under the stress and pressure of measuring up to external standards. It is a commonly held and age old philosophy that "we are human and we are here and thereby have innate value." Our existence has this innate value regardless of our degree of "success." If we do not accept ourselves as innately valuable, then our setbacks can be devastating and a useful and contented life will remain beyond our grasp. This is why addressing ourselves as winners or losers reinforces a ridiculous measurement. Though we all hold ourselves in disregard at times, if we continue to believe that our setbacks are an indication of our worth as a person, we will live sad and misguided lives. There are far too many of us who have been conditioned to believe we "must measure up" and succeed -- always in comparison to others. If we continue to do this, we create an emotional and spiritual emptiness which no amount of external success can cure. Therefore, measuring our worth by our unsuccessful attempts or criticizing ourselves for not doing what we "should" be doing only intensifies the obstacles we face in learning to live more abundantly. *These habits are absolutely self-defeating.*

We do not have to fall into this trap. We do not need to judge ourselves by external accomplishments and measurements that, by the nature of life, flow up and down. We can turn our mistakes and setbacks into great value by viewing them and ourselves differently.

FOCUS ON THE LESSONS

Setbacks and mistakes can teach us many lessons, if we care to learn them. By focusing our attention on what we might learn and what we could do differently, we increase our experience and wisdom -- which is invaluable in our future endeavors. If we never made any mistakes in our past, addressed and corrected them, we would be overwhelmed by any job or task that did not go perfectly. If we must always "get it right" it greatly impedes our ability to learn, adapt, and

Give Yourself a Raise

grow. Furthermore, if we are operating under the gun (anxious and frightened we will not do well), we are prone to make needless errors -- which undermines our confidence even more. We need to challenge the idea that mistakes and setbacks must be avoided. They cannot be. We need to view ourselves as being in the process of learning to perform effectively *on average*. Living under the tyranny of having to always do it right will make us lose sight of what we can learn from our experiences and can greatly diminish our view of our own capabilities.

We need to understand that everything we have experienced can be useful to us. We do not wish to repeat mistakes, of course. However, being human we often do. I have repeated the same mistakes with certain clients a dozen or more times until I learned that I needed to change a certain business policy. We are not stupid or hard headed. It is often just very difficult to break free from familiar patterns. We may experience setbacks of a similar nature many times before the lesson sinks in. If we are open to learning and changing, eventually we will not only correct the mistakes we have made but will move beyond the need to repeat self-defeating behavior.

When we take actions in areas where we lack experience, it is even more vital to allow ourselves to "do it imperfectly" and learn from our efforts along the way. If we can focus on the lessons that come from these experiences, we can adapt and give ourselves the ultimate chance to succeed. If we still do not prevail, we may learn to take new routes and establish new goals.

Lessons are invaluable. Lessons are also often painful. This is a fact of life. If we view experiences and lessons as valuable, they are. Instead, many of us tend to view them as hardship and subtly continue to present ourselves to others as victims of circumstance or bad luck. This is a dead end attitude resulting in dismal and depressing living. We need to be conscious of the trap of thinking this way and refrain from excessive self-pity and constantly portraying to others how difficult life is for us. If we have suffered mistreatment, injustice or bad luck, this does not mean we ignore it. It means we cannot continue to hold onto the pain of these incidents and let them subtly sabotage our efforts to live well. If difficult circumstances have befallen us, we must acknowledge the situation, experience our feelings about it, learn from it, and ultimately use it to motivate ourselves to do things differently. It may take a little time to get over some experiences, but we must make it our business to do so. In this way, we become inspirational role models for others and ourselves.

If we focus on the lessons and information garnered from our experiences, we will not be as hesitant to try again and again. We will see that our evolution is truly more important than the goal itself. As we learn, we can apply all of our past knowledge to present and future endeavors. Ultimately, this is why setbacks are such assets.

No Apology Needed

When we have not lived up to our own or others expectations, some of us get into the habit of apologizing for past experiences. This is a self-defeating process, if there ever was one. We may not exactly say, "I'm sorry." Yet, our demeanor and tone will tell others how embarrassed and ashamed we are that we did not have it together enough to succeed. Clients of mine have apologized for being fired, for taking time off to raise a family, for not passing an exam, for having a business go under, for not having addressed issues sooner, for being in debt, for not getting a particular job, for ending a relationship, and on and on and on.

If you harmed someone, you may need to apologize to that person. However, in the pursuit of your goals, *you do not need to apologize to anyone for the facts of your life*. We are all human. We have all fallen short of our goals at some time in our lives. Yet, the propensity to act as though we are less capable and not as worthy because of these setbacks is clearly an inaccurate depiction of ourselves. Why do we need to apologize for something every human being naturally experiences?

We do not need to indiscriminately tell others of our past difficulties. However, if asked *and* if appropriate, we should say what happened simply and directly without ever judging ourselves in tone or attitude. If we are to judge, then we might interpret the situation positively and say something like, "Yes, it was difficult at the time, but I learned so many valuable lessons from the experience that it added to my wisdom and skills." That, by the way, is the truth. It is through the correction of mistakes, and learning from experience, that enhance our abilities.

In my own case, it was the myriad of obstacles and challenges I faced that became invaluable experiences for me in my consulting business. My clients are the benefactors of my past difficulties. The knowledge of this makes me view my prior experiences with understanding, respect, and even gratitude.

BE AVERAGE, BE IMPERFECT, AND BE INCREDIBLY ABUNDANT

We do not have to reach our highest potential to be loved, valued, and accepted. We only need to attempt to discover what we need and want and move toward it. We will do so very imperfectly. Perfection is an illusion. Any adult with a modicum of maturity will tell you so. In a view shared by spiritual leaders the world over, it is our birthright to be imperfect yet enjoy the splendor this life has to give. This can be a wonderful concept to adopt. It means you can falter, fail, make attempts in an average way, and reap the vast benefits of moving imperfectly ahead.

We all know people who do not possess superior talent or skills and yet enjoy much in their lives. While it may seem they have been lucky, on some level they have allowed themselves to be average, imperfect, and enjoy a good life.

So many of us have impossible standards for ourselves and others. This sets us up for failure before we begin. Our setbacks then become disasters rather than valuable learning experiences. How can we have more abundance and feel more prosperous if we continue to criticize and demand perfection of ourselves? Make your mantra "Strive to be average." This means to move ahead moderately and consistently, allowing yourself to be human and make mistakes. Adapt as necessary, but take your time and lower your unrealistic standards so that your performance may rise.

This phrase is often said to beginners of some self-help programs: *The good news is -- you are just like everybody else. The bad news is -- you are just like everybody else.* In striving to be average and lowering our intense standards, we can feel a sense of accomplishment rather than failure. Also, if we let go of our rigid requirements, our unique qualities will come out. We are all different, of course, and our talents and personalities exist in a wonderful spectrum. In striving to be our average self, we can accept ourselves more easily and allow our distinct differences to come forth. If we continue to live as perfectionists, we hide our true human (imperfect) nature and may never appreciate ourselves and live as valuable, authentic human beings.

In allowing ourselves to be average, we let go of the impossible feat of having to always do it right, always succeed and never make mistakes. We can still work diligently at pursuing our dreams without expecting ourselves to live up to ridiculous standards or comparisons that we cannot meet. We need to lift this burden and enjoy a lighter, more fulfilling existence. By demanding ourselves to constantly function at high standards in an imperfect world, we are deprived of so many opportunities for contentment and success. We come to view our possessions, our experiences, and ourselves as inadequate. By striving to be average in our efforts and expectations, we give ourselves the chance to live humbly, abundantly, and happily.

Do you wish to keep your spirit low or learn to take life's difficult experiences in stride and even turn them into great value? In experiencing setbacks, it is not your initial feelings of disappointment or discouragement that matter. It is your overall view of the situation that determines whether you keep yourself down or accept your humanity and move ahead with greater understanding, experience, and appreciation of yourself.

—❈— HE TRANSFORMED HIS "FAILURES" INTO SUCCESS —❈—

Fired from his last job as an attorney, Bill had not worked in 18 months. Understandably, Bill was depressed and frustrated that his efforts to gain employment seemed at a dead end. His last job was in the public interest area as a legal advocate in discrimination cases. Though he had been on many job interviews in the prior year and a half, Bill believed the facts of his employment history gave him an almost insurmountable series of obstacles. How would he explain his employment "gap" (lack of work in the last 18 months)? He had failed the Bar exam not once, but twice -- passing on the third try. The position he had been dismissed from was his first job as an attorney, and he had little professional experience in the legal industry. At the age of 34, he was also older than most beginning attorneys, because, before attending law school, he had worked for a major corporation for several years. He also felt that as a member of an ethnic minority group it would be more challenging to get into "white" firms. With these obstacles on his mind, Bill was going into interviews with defensive and self-defeating attitudes.

His wife worked full-time, but the family was straining financially. Bill spent much time caring for their two young sons because child care was another expense he felt they could not afford. Since there was less time to look for work, this further impeded his job search. Not knowing how to change his situation, he attended one of my workshops and then became a private client.

—◇◇◇—

Bill had a simple, but not easily resolvable, problem. He had adopted negative attitudes and judgments about himself and his circumstances. This was the crux of Bill's difficulties. He assumed his judgments about himself were the judgments of all prospective employers, and he went to look for work with these self-defeating beliefs. In other words, Bill was acting on his own negative view of his history and experiences. This perpetuated a self-fulfilling prophecy. Not surprisingly, as he endeavored to find a job a vicious cycle of poor results and a more negative attitude followed.

Having been fired, Bill saw himself as a failure. He heaped on other negative judgments because he had not worked for 18 months <u>and</u> because he took three times to pass the Bar exam <u>and</u> because his wife was the current breadwinner <u>and</u> because he was possibly too old <u>and</u> fighting an uphill battle as a minority. This viewpoint was overwhelming and would be to anyone. These kinds of negative assessments are far too common among many of us.

Within a few weeks of our working together, in his interviews Bill decided to stop apologizing for his past and present circumstances. He refused to communicate in tone or meaning that his work history was a problem. If asked, we decided Bill would be honest without being critical of his professional experiences. Over time, Bill and I kept pursuing new avenues of possible work. In each case, he would report to me his experiences and we would discuss his attitude, his responses to interview questions and approaches for the next series of actions.

Bill wanted to feel like a lawyer again and also generate income. An opportunity surfaced to take a part-time, temporary job assisting an attorney in private practice. He did not like the work too much, which was an improvement in his attitude. It meant he was valuing himself much more. How can any of us satisfy ourselves in an unfulfilling situation? The job search continued. Throughout this process, I kept encouraging him to proceed moderately and consistently, allowing himself to be imperfect and make mistakes along the way.

After working with me for a year, Bill accepted a position as an attorney with a charitable organization. The organization provided legal services for individuals who suffer from discrimination. Isn't it ironic that Bill got a job helping others who face discrimination by lifting his own "self-discrimination"?

Over time, I had encouraged Bill to talk about his experiences in new ways. Bill developed the skill of speaking of himself favorably. He learned to talk about his work and life experiences (setbacks) as assets -- not liabilities. He could explain, without apologizing, his strengths and weaknesses.

1) **Taking the Bar exam three times.** His original view: failure, lack of intelligence, fear that he was in the wrong profession. The new view: he had developed the traits of courage, persistence, and stamina when faced with a difficult challenge and continued on to success.

2) **18 months without being employed.** His original view: made him undesirable to firms, showed lack of employability, and made him inadequate as a professional. The new view: gave him the luxury of time to explore and research the marketplace. This allowed him to reassess his needs and proceed in his job search with clarity and purpose.

3) **Being fired.** His original view: showed him as being unqualified and a bad risk. The new view: regarded it as a learning experience in which he could view his mistakes as an opportunity for growth and future success. (In talking about this, I encouraged him to quote Henry Ford, and other successful individuals, on the necessity of setbacks in attaining ultimate achievement.)

4) **On not having much professional experience and being older than the average starting attorney.** The original view: he would not be taken seriously, he would be looking for a job and a salary that is only appropriate for "kids." The new view: Isn't it absolutely fabulous that he decided to pursue his vision and work in a profession that he originally did not believe was possible? He allowed himself to go after it and get the training he needed rather than stay in another field that made him unhappy. Of course, he was satisfied to begin at a salary that was entry-level because his investment was in long-term success and satisfaction in his field. Being older gave him a level of life experience and maturity that could only aid him in dealing with clients and situations that a younger person might not understand.

5) **On being a minority individual.** His original view: most firms or organizations do not really want minority attorneys. They may fear the

ethnic differences. They may believe a minority person may "turn off" certain individuals who think white attorneys appear more qualified. Also, there is a perception by many that minority attorneys have an axe to grind. The new view: Being a minority gave him a unique perspective on issues of discrimination that he often faced himself. He viewed himself as a proponent of equality, not special treatment for any person, whether they are Black, White, Hispanic, Indian, or Asian. As a member of a minority he could be a role model for other persons of his race by practicing a philosophy of justice for everyone. Clients and colleagues would innately come to trust his fairness and depend upon his skills which would help break negative stereotypes.

When Bill began to see and reinforce the positive view of his challenges and setbacks, his sincere and forthright attitude came out and his honesty was compelling. I believe this is what eventually landed him this job. It is certainly true that some prospective employers, maybe even most, would hold the negative view of some of Bill's circumstances. The point is: if Bill held the negative view as true, then everyone else would believe <u>his</u> negative version of the facts. Before, Bill's attitudes were self-sabotaging. He kept himself from getting a job by agreeing with many negative interpretations. When he worked at changing them, he convinced others (and himself) of his value. Everyone did not have to agree with Bill's more positive view of his circumstances; only one employer needed to do that. He discovered he did not need general acceptance of his positive views, but specific opportunities with more positive, intelligent, and open-minded individuals.

Bill's position was entry-level, but this was only his second job in the legal field, and his first as a full-time attorney after passing the Bar exam. The exposure he is now receiving is a wonderful investment in his future. Although his salary was modest at the beginning, his wife was pleased to have another income in the family. Bill was quite pleased to get work he believed in while gaining the professional experience he needed to launch his career. Of equal significance was the way he obtained this position. It strengthened his sense that he can make mistakes, learn from them, and still be a capable attorney -- imperfect and very valuable.

Bill's prior professional experiences were quite painful to him. With help, he was able to acknowledge and confront these experiences. After we began working together, he still felt like apologizing for himself but portrayed the positive view of his circumstances, "acting as if" the positive view was the correct view. Despite feeling frustrated and doubtful this *would work, Bill kept at it and inevitably convinced himself that his setbacks and prior experiences were assets that would serve him -- which they did and which they shall continue to do.*

REMINDERS:

- You can turn your setbacks and mistakes into priceless assets by focusing on the lessons you can learn from them.

- You do not need to apologize to anyone for your less-than-successful endeavors.

- You can praise yourself for the wisdom you gain by going through difficult times.

- When setbacks occur, you can allow yourself to feel the natural disappointment and discouragement without giving up on your hopes and dreams.

- You can choose the positive interpretation of the events you have experienced and your circumstances as the truth.

- You can proceed in an average way, be imperfect, falter, and also enjoy great abundance.

Give Yourself a Raise

APPLY PERSEVERANCE

CHAPTER 16

Babe Ruth hit 714 home runs. He struck out 1,330 times.
The Baseball Encyclopedia

Persistence, dedication, drive, and perseverance -- these words conjure up similar images. They point to the idea of taking action consistently over a course of time. It is a simple truth that perseverance works. It does not always work to attain every specific goal, but *as a principle* it works.

Taking action consistently, with serious intent, persuades people to see you differently than others who make a less committed effort. Persevering allows you to tap into resources you would not have otherwise seen. Consistency of action helps you develop much more experience and knowledge about the goals you seek, your wants and needs, and your strengths and weaknesses.

Perseverance, directed positively, is probably the most compelling professional quality one can develop. A person who pursues their desires with inner-determination exudes confidence that attracts others. Perseverance as a quality inspires us and motivates us. We want to be around it and have it rub off on us. Developing and applying perseverance to our goals may be the only difference between experiencing a stimulating and fulfilling life or desperate and painful mediocrity.

The changes that can result from persistent action are unlimited. For example, Thomas Edison was once questioned about his experiments to find a durable filament for the light bulb. It was related

related in an Edison biography that he conducted over 10,000 separate experiments (that's right TEN THOUSAND) before he finally discovered a metal alloy that worked effectively. With his success, the incandescent light bulb was born. This invention changed the course of history for every person, company, economy, and country on the face of the planet. A reporter asked him how he could keep going after TEN THOUSAND failures at not finding the right filament. Mr. Edison replied that he did not have 10,000 failures but had 10,000 successes at finding out what did not work.

Certainly, it would be extreme to suggest that any of us apply this level of perseverance. This story illustrates how the character and quality of our lives can be altered immensely by a desire to develop and apply this trait.

Here are a few observations for your consideration regarding the quality or trait we come to experience as perseverance.

PURSUING GOALS OF SUBSTANCE

Perseverance needs to be aimed at self-nurturing dreams and desires. Pursuing goals motivated by self-importance, superficial image, approval from others, gaining control over people, etc., will only drain, not strengthen, your character and internal stamina. Even upon attainment of this kind of goal, you can feel quite empty and disillusioned. In other words, if your goal is based only on overcompensating for your insecurities or negative feelings about yourself, you are likely to fall far short of rewarding experiences and inner satisfaction. Perseverance also tends to break down before or after reaching goals that are primarily superficial or glory-driven achievements. We all know stories of hardworking celebrities who "had it all" only to experience constant and extreme anxiety with a final destination of addiction, violence, and even death. Also, we all know of people who focus on outer appearances and portraying images while they live in denial and despair. It is normal to have an external image of what you would like to accomplish or possess. It is only suggested that you check your underlying motives.

Is your goal for your own sense of accomplishment or do you primarily want the validation of others? If you want more money simply to enjoy material wealth or to take time off, do you envision maintaining a sense of purpose that involves service and interaction with others? Or do you see it as a way to escape the challenges of life? Do you see success as getting your own way and putting you in control over others, or as giving you a chance to pursue a vision and motivating others to join you in something worthwhile? Take another look.

Are your desires coming from a place where you want to express and enjoy your gifts and eventually share them with others? Or are they coming from a need to heal painful experiences so you will feel acceptable, lovable, and worthy (which you may fear you do not)? Just question your motives. The pursuit of purely self-centered goals and achievement of external "success" cannot heal inner wounds that only a dedication to self-discovery, growth, and living differently can mend.

All of us want approval and validation from others. Yet, if we pursue our goals knowing that our efforts and *our own approval* are what count, then it is likely our motives are coming from self-expression and self-care. In this respect, no matter what the outcome of your efforts, you will grow and ultimately succeed. Perseverance is made easier by thoughtfully examining the substance of your goals.

ACCEPT TIME

Try not to control time and it will take you along at the pace you need to go.

The greatest frustration for many of us is that we cannot control how long things take to transpire. We cannot move traffic, lose weight, or pay off our debts fast enough. Time always goes at its own speed. We may believe we are in a crisis and that a time deadline hangs over us. Only once in a great while is a deadline real. Most deadlines are man-made illusions. Even when a deadline is urgent and real, we still cannot control how long something takes to accomplish any more than we can control how long it is going to rain or how long a tree takes to grow.

In this society we have come up with the illusion that faster is better. There is a great fallacy in this society that pushing harder makes us more productive, that speed is good, and accomplishing more means better living. This actually robs us of quality of life. If this is you, I would kindly suggest that you begin to challenge the mania to "get it done faster." How can you enjoy the scenery if you are going 90 miles an hour down the road? If you like speed, take a fast ride now and again, but *you cannot fight time*. You will only make yourself frustrated and deeply unhappy in doing so. Indeed, time is like a patient parent trying to slow you down so that you may discover and enjoy the myriad of opportunities and gifts this life offers. Perseverance can erode and break down when trying to force results and solutions in too little time.

If others try to use time to control you, go back and reread Chapter 8, "Prepare Yourself to Act on Better Opportunities." It is too difficult to enjoy life if you are influenced by someone who misuses time to torture themselves.

This does not mean you should get rid of time-saving conveniences. It means if you focus on finishing, getting there faster, and driving ahead, your future will feel exactly as stressful as your present. You will soon be pushing again from the "new" level you have reached.

Our lives are a work in progress. It's finished when you can't draw breath. It is our challenge to learn to accept and enjoy the passage of time rather than be a slave to it. Perseverance only works in cooperation with time. Professional or personal growth requires moderate and consistent effort, not speed and force of will. In this culture, it may not be easy, but you can decide to accept that things take time. This can give you a sense of balance and completion. If you race through your days and your life as if you were running to catch a train, you will eventually become drained and disillusioned and won't enjoy where you're going, even if you get there.

Asking For Help

I do not know of a single person who does not need help. If we are to persevere, we must at some point get assistance from others. For those of us who feel as though we may be burdensome or that we are not entitled to the aid and attention of others, this is a challenge. Asking for help must go hand in hand with making what you want important. If it is your decision to make something important, then it is important enough for others to consider it seriously.

Since we are only human, we cannot conceive of and carry out every possible option. Simple logic dictates, then, we must ask for help. This can be a very loaded emotional issue for many of us. It requires that we face possible rejection from one or more persons. It often requires that we become honest and vulnerable in making requests.

It also requires that we allow ourselves to accept the generosity and graciousness of others. If we believe what we want does not really matter, or that we do not deserve to attain our goals, or that our needs are unreasonable, accepting help can be painful. This may go against long-held thinking expressed in the belief "I should not need anybody to help me." Yet, if we can bear the discomfort of asking for help, we will eventually receive it. If we do this enough, we can dismiss the negative notion that we do not need or deserve the time and attention of others.

Asking for help is prosperous. Going it alone in pursuing our desires will not only crush our ability to persevere, it is incredibly self-depriving. Face whatever fear you have and begin to ask others for help, even if they seem to have nothing to gain by helping you. In reality, they gain by giving and by making a positive connection with you.

There is no such thing as becoming successful alone. We need others to succeed -- to support us, give us ideas, keep us focused, use our services, etc. Without the help of others, we cannot truly thrive and flourish, and why would we want to?

Focus on Action as the Result

Part of learning to apply perseverance is learning to assess triumph. To repeat an idea from a prior chapter, you can adopt the idea that triumph is in your efforts rather than in results. If you are constantly succeeding because effort is success, then you are always successful by taking action. If you are always successful, it is vastly easier to keep up the good work.

I praise my clients CONSTANTLY for their EFFORTS. Even when their results are quite pleasing to them, I first praise them for their attempts. I know all of their attempts will not end in positive results. Are we only to judge ourselves by our efforts that turn out well? If we only measure ourselves by our achievements alone, we can agonize over every action, every step, and every attempt we make to just get along in the world. This imprisons our spirits and diminishes our healthy desires. Praising our efforts makes us internally powerful and confident. We will learn it often takes many small efforts (many of which won't work at all) to eventually attain a good result. This is not hardship. This is fine and good, if we view efforts as wonderful in and of themselves for our well-being.

Therefore, make taking actions the result. In other words, making an effort is the result on which to focus. Then outcomes happen as a by-product of action, not as the direct effect. Remember, sometimes when you polish it here, it shines over there.

Praise yourself for each and every effort you make, great or small. Each attempt is a genuine success. Thomas Edison thought so. Appreciating your smallest steps will give you the sense you are making progress. This will build confidence and esteem and make persevering much easier.

COPING WITH NEGATIVE MESSAGES

We all receive messages to give up and quit. Some messages heard from others or emanate from our own thinking are: "Who do you think you are?" "You're never going to get what you want." "You don't deserve it anyway." "If they only knew what you were really like, they would never consider you." "What's the use?" "You are too old, young, tall, short, fat, skinny, inexperienced, over-qualified." "There is too much competition." "The economy is terrible." "You are too smart for this job." "You can't want THAT!" "What will others think if you do that?" "It's too hard." "Why do I have to work?" "Nobody really cares anyway." "I don't have any employable skills." "I am not going to take a job that's beneath me." "Look what I'll have to put up with." "Everybody in that business is nuts." "I hate doing this kind of work." "I want to do it, but I am terrible at _____ (fill in the blank)." "There's no money for that." "I don't have the right clothes, education, looks, temperament, resume." "After I lose weight, get married, pay off my debts, get more training, the economy gets a little better, get the kids off to college, get my Christmas bonus, wait for the company to relocate, get divorced, after my dental work is done, then I can try to do something about this." "Look at it out there. You're better off where you are." "I'm too confused." "I'm too particular." "You can't do it." "Why are you even trying to do it?" "What did I do in the past to deserve this crap." "Life sucks and then you die."

Maybe we will all be better in the next life, but we may have to spend a lot of time in this one before then. So, while we are here, we might as well deal with the negativity each of us experiences at some point. These negative thoughts can come from us or, unfortunately, from others.

Here are three effective ways to address the negativity that can keep us from moving outward and enjoying greater prosperity in our lives. (1) Even though we cannot eliminate our own and others' negative thoughts, we can remove ourselves as much as possible from negative influences. (2) We can visualize success. (3) We only need to keep moving our muscles to take action despite how "loud" the voices become that would have us stop.

Some negative thoughts will continue no matter what we do. We are human and this is natural. We will question ourselves, no matter how confident we become. Do not expect that you will proceed and become abundant without experiencing negative thoughts. This is when we need to strive to remember and have our friends remind us of secure thoughts. We need to reassure ourselves and seek comfort, rationality and guidance to balance the part of us that is uncertain and insecure. In part, that is what this book is about -- striving for balance so we can move ahead, while accepting our insecurities and imperfections, and still enjoy overall satisfaction and success.

We cannot eliminate any part of the spectrum of human inner experience. Nor would that be desirable. At times, it is the critical voice that keeps us from doing something self-destructive. This is why we need to ask others for help and guidance, no matter how self-sufficient we become, to distinguish the healthy voice that is assessing a situation from the critical voice that undermines us.

To lessen the impact of negativity, remove yourself from these influences by turning off the TV, turning the page of a newspaper or magazine, getting off the phone, ending a personal conversation or anything that reinforces (a) the idea that you are not capable, (b) the odds of reaching your goals are nearly impossible due to society, the economy, or circumstances beyond your control, or (c) your goals will not give you enough even if you attain them. This is simple to say, but difficult to practice. You can, however, learn to do it. Negativity feeds on itself, growing the more we pay attention to it. Let yourself "turn off this noise." With practice you will get much better at leaving or ignoring those who espouse the dark view of a situation.

You can also visualize success by using your imagination to see yourself handling situations or specific scenarios thoughtfully and calmly. In visualizing success, you do not need to have the outcome work out in a positive or specific way. You only need to see yourself as calm, capable, and pursuing your goals with a positive outlook. Try this. It really works. After all, negative influences and messages play upon our imagination with images of discouragement, failure, and even disaster. Those negative pictures in our minds can govern our actions (or lack of actions) and create a negative self-fulfilling prophecy. If you practice seeing yourself in positive images and pictures in your mind, they too can govern your actions and lead you to a positive self-fulfilling prophecy. In using your imagination in this way, always put yourself in the picture and see yourself feeling poised, confident and capable. You may wish to buy the booklet Creative Visualization by Shakti Gawain. This short book can be incredibly helpful in using your imagination with powerful results. (see Resources in the back of this book).

Another extremely effective antidote to dealing with negative influences is to MOVE YOUR MUSCLES -- not obey your brain. Once you have determined a course of action, literally, let your muscles carry out the tasks. Your leg muscles, your arm muscles, your speech muscles are all controllable. Let your feet, hands and mouth do the work. Your brain may be working against you sometimes. Your muscles and your body can be commanded to overcome any negative thoughts and fears that would stop you from moving ahead. This is a principle that has been practiced with great effect by the patients and pupils of Dr. Abraham Low, founder of Recovery, Inc. in Chicago, Illinois. Dr. Low discovered that he could help patients overcome and even eliminate severe nervous symptoms and anxiety disorders (even for people who had were deemed to be hopeless neurotic cases) by teaching them to practice moving their muscles while bearing emotional discomfort. (See the Resources information in the back of this book for more information.)

In his book Mental Health Through Will Training, Dr. Low states "Nothing is more convincing than muscular performance." I have used this principle to help clients who otherwise could not take action due to the fear and negativity they were experiencing. Commanding your muscles to carry out a task you fear or hate to do will show you there is no danger in making efforts. This is extremely helpful when you are feeling confused, angry, or scared about moving forward. It does not even matter if the whole time you are taking an action you say to yourself, "Why bother? Why bother? This is dumb. What am I doing this for anyway? Why bother." You can act (move your muscles) *anyway*.

Controlling your muscles also includes refraining from action. As discussed earlier, we can remove ourselves from outer influences that reinforce our own negative thinking. We can cease doing anything that makes us feel worse about our chances "out there." We can cease moving so fast, trying to be extremely productive, and simply stop and let ourselves rest for a while. If we are racing, there is probably some fear or negative voice driving us.

We do not have to totally eliminate negativity. That would be impossible. We only need to learn to diminish it and act *in opposition* to it.

Rest and Leisure

You must take time to rest and do leisurely activities. To put it another way, you must take time to do leisurely activities and rest. Most importantly, take time off to rest and do leisurely activities.

Has the point been made?

You cannot prosper if you do not stop to enjoy what you already have and take time to nurture yourself. You must regularly treat yourself well -- including time when you demand absolutely nothing of yourself.

No one does this perfectly. At times, we all put out too much effort or focus on completing tasks without taking a break. However, if you do not allow yourself to slow down and stop at times, there can be no enjoyment in your efforts. Prosperity and constant stress are incompatible. You do not need to kill yourself to prosper. Quite the contrary, you will be much more contented if you relax, rest, and let things unfold without any effort on your part for a while.

Proceed at a moderate pace, then stop for a while. Proceed again when you feel a little (or a lot more) refreshed and renewed. Otherwise, you will diminish your capacity to help yourself if you are constantly stressed and drained. If you cannot slow down, you will eventually burn out -- and how can you continue effectively then?

Driving yourself endlessly is *not* perseverance; it is self-sabotage. It is trying to control outcomes or control time. Perseverance requires that you let efforts in pursuing your goals be followed by periods of "down time." If you are always tired, anxious, feeling driven, and never seem to feel rested, you probably need to slow down. You may need the support and assistance of others, friends and professionals alike, to accomplish this. Avail yourself of this help, if needed.

You cannot live abundantly by rushing through your goals like a freight train that never stops. Water the flower and let it grow. Stand back and enjoy the flower for a while; and then go do something else or just take a break. You will come back to water it another time. Take a stroll. Take a nap. Go to a favorite museum. See a movie -- even in the middle of a work day! Watch a favorite TV show. Read something enjoyable. Plan for, save for, and take a *real* vacation -- not one where you have to stay with friends and relatives. Take a day off from work and DO NOTHING work related or that takes intense effort.

Without rest, leisure, and relaxation, we cannot replenish ourselves. In that case, no matter what we have gained, our abundance is in danger of being lost or it will give us little joy in having it -- that is, if we can get anywhere at all by running ourselves into the ground.

Moderate and consistent action is transforming, but remember to take time to rest and relax. Combining these philosophies can yield gentle yet incredibly powerful results that can make the difference between glorious and mediocre living.

It is important to understand that most of us will face both practical and emotional obstacles in moving ahead. Perseverance works to overcome them. The ideas discussed in this chapter are meant to give you more tools for confronting the challenges that would keep you from staying on your path toward abundance. In using them, you will find a greater sense of self-esteem, self-acceptance, and a reinvigoration of spirit.

Developing and applying perseverance allows us to become more spiritual beings, if we are open to it. We begin to trust that life will inevitably give us what we need to survive and thrive. If we apply perseverance to goals that are truly nourishing for us, we gain the inner knowledge that we are right with the world. We find we do not need to work so hard and rest and relaxation actually helps us accomplish more. We come to understand that *everything* we experience becomes part of our imperfect and magnificent humanity and *everything* we receive can be seen as a blessing.

Slow and Steady Effort Helped Him Win the Race

Twenty-three years as a city government official in Dallas came to an abrupt end for one of my clients. A newly elected mayor placed one of his own people in Carl's position which was thought to be a "safe" position -- free from partisan politics. Carl's long, distinguished career and experience as a financial planner did not spare him from the challenges and anxiety of being out of work. He was a family man with a teenage daughter at home and another daughter he was supporting at college. He had a mortgage, car payments, and many other financial responsibilities. His wife worked but could not solely support the family for any substantial length of time. I first met Carl when he attended one of my workshops on making job transitions while he was in New York visiting relatives. He was nervous about money, for obvious reasons, and wanted my opinion about how to find a job quickly to prevent a lapse in income.

Getting fired, or having a major drop in income, is traumatic for anyone. The shock of losing work and the desire to fix the problem quickly was understandable, but it was not in Carl's best interests. I suggested we thoughtfully consider his current situation and continue to work together by telephone and in person whenever he was in New York.

The first task I wanted to accomplish with Carl, as it is with many of my new clients, was to slow the process down. It is almost impossible to make effective decisions under extreme pressure. Acting out of fear and panic leads to self-defeat. At first, we looked at his entire financial situation, including all of his financial resources. We discovered that Carl did have more options financially than immediately apparent. Out of fear and without looking squarely at the facts, Carl had set an arbitrary date to get a job. This is a fairly common mistake, but based on the current reality of his resources, we moved this date back by six months. In almost every case, more time equals more options. This did not mean that Carl could not find a job in less than six months. It meant that we had time to create and implement a plan of consistent and moderate action. In discussing this decision, Carl experienced instant stress relief. He came to quickly understand that he did not need to jump at the first job. At this point, the work of assessing what he needed in a new job, and a plan of action to attain it, became possible.

Carl realized that many aspects of his position with the city were unsatisfactory. As a city official he was required to live within the city limits. However, he and his wife had long wanted to move into a safer, quieter neighborhood in the suburbs. In addition, strictly governed salaries could only increase minimally every year. There were no bonuses for his position no matter how effective his performance. In going through his options, we determined it would be much better for him to work for a private corporation rather than in the public service.

Frequently, it can take a long time to find new employment. With the level of salary Carl was seeking, the process could take longer still. Employers take more time to fill higher level positions. Once Carl accepted this, we talked about the kind of position he should look for, and how to approach his job search overall. The subject of perseverance came up. Certainly, Carl wanted to find employment sooner than later, but I asked if he was willing to take time, if necessary. It is vital to understand that our goals may require consistency of effort to be accomplished. We had already taken a realistic view of his financial situation, had discussed his motives for the kind of position he wanted. Now I was suggesting that he be open to a slow and methodical job search. Though he was not thrilled with this prospect, in principle, he agreed.

Together, we came up with a number of approaches to finding long-term employment. I was impressed with Carl's progress in asserting himself. Over the course of several months, he sent resumes, made phone calls, went to lunches, and secured interviews. He came close to being hired on two occasions, but it did not work out. After months of job searching, this left him discouraged, angry and confused. This was exactly when he needed to apply perseverance. This was the point at which many individuals drag their feet, procrastinate or give up all together. We needed to draw upon a number of tools to help Carl avoid this trap. These tools included, making new actions the goals in and of themselves, praising himself for each action taken (no matter how small), reminding himself of the underlying positive substance of his goals, and simply commanding his muscles to carry out a task even when he felt angry or discouraged. I further encouraged him to *do only a few actions a day and then stop to rest or do something pleasurable for himself.*

Though it was difficult, by using these tools Carl was able to keep moving ahead at a moderate pace. He was developing and applying perseverance. He discovered he had more stamina than he thought.

After several more weeks of action, we agreed he should try to earn temporary income as he continued his job search. Putting his mind to the task, he found work as a "temp" employee as financial analyst at a major realty company. The project he was working on, however, was not temporary but might take more than a year to complete. Carl was paid through a temporary agency but after two months, we decided that Carl should attempt to gain permanent employment with the realty company. It took patience and fortitude to navigate through the corporate maze. A number of strategies were carried out over many months. Carl asked for help, and eventually made his desires known on a regular basis. Though the process frustrated him at times, he did not push to make something happen quickly, even when mistakes were made or no results were happening. This was a major triumph.

It took nearly a year, but the process paid off. While earning an income as a temporary worker and taking proactive (painstaking at times) steps, Carl accepted employment as an officer of the company. Over the course of the year (while he was earning a full-time income), Carl asserted himself with determination and an outwardly confident attitude. In doing so, he earned his own and others respect. His initial salary increased more than 20% over his previous city job, plus an added bonus of $12,000 in his first full year. He and his wife have moved out of the city and are thrilled with their new home. He finds his new work both challenging and satisfying, and there is much room for upward mobility in the organization. Carl got everything he wanted and more.

Upon being fired from his previous job, Carl did not have real plans. He only had what he believed to be an urgent situation. In our work together, we found that he could take action thoughtfully. He further developed the habit of asserting himself to a much greater degree. Through perseverance, he ultimately enjoyed the rewards of this new attitude. Though there was never any guarantee his actions would result in a permanent position that met his needs, Carl learned to keep moving toward his goal (despite many frustrating experiences) and operate with solid motives and actions to move ahead. The way he conducted himself would have inevitably led him to some reasonable opportunity. If Carl continues to apply these sound principles, he will give himself a much better chance to advance in his company and enjoy his personal life and his growing abundance to a greater degree.

REMINDERS:

- Moderate and consistent effort will transform your attitudes and your circumstances.

- Approach your goals with healthy motives.

- Constantly rushing around depletes and deprives you. Accept that things take time.

- Keep asking for help to keep yourself going. You will get it and you deserve it.

- You can remove yourself from negative influences.

- You can use your imagination to visualize conducting yourself successfully.

- When scared or confused, you can command your muscles to move to complete actions.

- You can overcome the negative thinking of your brain and convince yourself there is no danger and no reason to stop moving toward your goal.

- You deserve to rest, relax, and keep your spirit refreshed.

- As often as possible, do something good for yourself.

ALLOW YOURSELF TO BE PROSPEROUS

CHAPTER 17

No one can give you what you deny yourself.
Kai Opaka

When I first began to change my actions and the methods of managing my money, I did so by rote. I was following the guidance and suggestions of others who were more experienced than I. Rarely did I question their input because I sincerely wished to discontinue the confusion, frustration, and vicious cycle of deprivation in which I found myself. The pain of my unmanageable situation made it easier for me to try new approaches without really understanding if, or how, they would work. In time, these new approaches created positive changes and began to make more sense to me. I was happy to see progress, but I did not yet *internally* experience the benefits. In other words, even when better things were happening, I frequently felt pained and afraid. There were fears of losing what I had just attained, of falling backward again, and that things would not change in the long run. There was also the pain from acting against old behaviors that had long been entrenched in the way I handled my money and my life. What I came to realize was that these intense feelings (and the beliefs that illicit them) were the reasons why I lived with such deprivation. Because of this I could not have lived abundantly, no matter what actions I took. As I changed my behaviors and actions, acting upon new beliefs (acting *as if* I believed them most of the time), the positive changes that occurred brought up feelings of agitation and fright. I came to realize I was terrified of letting myself be prosperous. To experience growth and abundance was not familiar to me at all. Stress, struggle, and strain had always been my overriding reality. It became apparent that most of the new behaviors and methods I was employing made simple common sense, but this flew in the face of my long-held, self-denying beliefs. Before I became truly ready to change, emotionally I just could not, or did not, allow myself to partake of abundance -- which was always there. My previous, familiar reality was too threatened. It was the guidance, wisdom, and encouragement from others who had been down a similar path that made the difference and helped me slowly move in a new direction.

Those of us who have life experience marked by a great deal of stress and strain have operated under a host of false assumptions. If we had difficultly getting our needs met, we assume what we want is far from our reach, believing we need to expend ourselves totally to just maintain ourselves, let alone obtain the good things of life. Our training set us up to expect and find hardship, and we do. Once we realize we learned false lessons, we can challenge the myth that life is a continual struggle. We can prepare ourselves to have greater prosperity. With a new view, we can learn to experience this wonderful paradox: we do not have to push to "get" everything; we only need to allow abundance to come into our consciousness and act gently to let it in. Yes, we need to make effort but we must learn to stand back and let our actions take root. We can learn to let ourselves wait for things to grow or come to us -- not wrestle them away from life, often in utter futility.

There is a vast difference between healthy effort and intense strain. We can learn to receive things much more easily, though our past experiences may have taught us not to expect this or that we do not deserve to have good things come to us without straining. As we change our behavior based on new beliefs, greater prosperity will come to us much more readily. There have probably been countless times when something good has been right in front of us, but we were unwilling, or unable, to partake of it. It happens far more often than we even imagine. As you practice these principles, that is going to change.

Allowing yourself to be prosperous is not about straining with intense effort; it is about taking self-caring actions with moderation and consistency and letting abundance come to you. This is why it is repeated throughout this book how important it is *just to consider these ideas* before taking action. Thinking is the preparation for action, and it is also the preparation for accepting abundance once it comes. More abundance exists for you right now, today. You only need to give yourself permission to let it in. You do this by acting as though you deserve prosperity and abundance. Then, you will have them. How do you act as though you deserve the good things in life? Follow and practice the principles and ideas in this book that have inspired you. You will eventually feel you do deserve the best from life.

LETTING GO OF STRUGGLE AND STRAIN

There has been much discussion throughout this book of overcoming obstacles, facing difficulties and bearing the discomfort of distressing feelings while moving ahead. While we may need to address the very real challenges that will surface in our efforts to enjoy more abundant living, it is a trap to believe that we *must* struggle. We may be so indoctrinated to living in adversity, we create unnecessary difficulties, drama and suffering for ourselves. Allowing ourselves to be prosperous carries with it the bright promise that we do not always have to work so hard to have abundance.

When we become adept at practicing principles of prosperity, it is amazing how little effort it may take for things to go well. Struggle is something we all face, but it is not something that must accompany all our endeavors. The professional baseball player creates excitement in the way he hits, throws, fields, and plays the game. To us, his skill and grace seem effortless. After years of practice, it almost becomes so. His methodical approach to practice and his trust in his own abilities does make his game easier and smoother. He can simply enjoy his talents without straining and receive all the wonderful benefits of his professional skill.

In the same way, we need to be prepared to pursue our goals and practice new methods, learning and adapting as we go. Even though certain obstacles could be challenging, we do not need to expect things to be difficult. In thinking every action and every plan will take incredible determination, we insure we will have a challenging time of it. In reality, as we take action moderately and consistently, we can anticipate things happening more easily.

As we move ahead, we need to remind ourselves to challenge the fallacies we may have once believed. If things happen easily, we do deserve it. We can have many prosperous things happen to us without intense effort and strain.

Certainly, we will face problems. All of us are handed things in life that are difficult and unfair. Likewise, all of us get breaks that come without hardship. We do not need to judge either of these types of occurrences. In letting go of struggle, we say to ourselves, "Yes, I will do what is necessary -- even if what is necessary is to do nothing, let things unfold and accept prosperity without much effort on my part."

In perpetuating struggle, we almost always take a fighting and adversarial position against ourselves and others. In letting go of struggle, we refuse to fight to get our needs met from any one source or force results in a certain time frame. We do not need to flail against a storm of obstacles with *grim* determination. Instead, we can take another route, seek a solution that gives us a sense of balance and decide not to fight circumstances. In response to telephone busy signals, we do not have to keep dialing fifteen times in a row. We can choose to stop dialing after two or three times and try later or on another day. If we cannot seem to get through, we can contact the party in another way. If we are to eliminate the feeling that life is a continual struggle, we may even need to terminate contact with individuals with whom we expend a lot of effort (cannot get "on the line") to maintain a relationship.

Struggle is an inherent part of learning and living. It is not, however, a condition that hangs over us like a black cloud. Struggle exists for positive reasons. It helps us grow by teaching us to become resourceful and overcome obstacles. What is meant here by letting go of struggle is letting go of the notion that you must always fight and intensely exert yourself to get your needs met. In other words, letting go of struggle means giving up fighting as the way to pursue your goals. An on-going intense effort to get your needs met is contrary to living abundantly.

Once, I was searching for a site to hold a career conference. I looked at a number of hotels with conference facilities. The space I wanted to rent was a state-of-the-art conference center. In my view it was modern, majestic and indicative of the abundance I wanted everyone to be thinking about. The rental for the day was higher than most of my other options -- $10,000 for the day -- but I thought I needed it. The only other hotel that was a good possibility was across town. It was an older, more classic hotel -- not nearly as modern and new. It was nice but did not suit my image of the conference. The cost for it was only $2,000 for the day. I had decided on the modern facility, and I made a number of calls and sent several telefaxes to the hotel sales department. The hotel sales representative returned only one of my calls and I was out at the time. I became angrier and angrier with each attempt to get through to him. "What's wrong with these people? Don't they need business? Don't they want my money?" I kept trying. Meanwhile, the sales manager of the older hotel kept calling ME. He was trying to woo me. He took me to lunch, outlined how he could make my conference more successful, asked if there were any special needs he could help me with. He was thoroughly attentive and professional. But I spent a month trying to contact the newer, more expensive hotel -- my first choice.

Why had I been struggling so? Because struggle is something that was familiar and, I had always thought, was a part of anything I did. I was fighting and pounding my head against a wall and getting angry and depressed. This was something I had done on countless occasions in my life. I was trying to get someone to show up who just wasn't available.

Because I was learning to do things differently, suddenly I *woke up*. I stopped fighting and let go of my "first choice." Since the fighting and struggle stopped, the agitation soon dissipated. I immediately called the sales manager from the older hotel and within a few days contracted to use their space. As it turned out, the participants loved the classic quality of the older architecture. The hotel staff made running the event much easier than I thought possible. To a person, the staff was courteous, efficient and professional. The final outcome was a great success. I charged admission to this conference. If I had taken the space for $10,000 I would have suffered a loss of several thousand dollars. With the older, classic hotel I made a nice profit for the day and valuable contacts. If I kept struggling (fighting), I may have eventually gotten the new hotel to cooperate and would have hurt myself in the process. I was thankful I was able to let go of struggling and let prosperity in.

We do not need to brace ourselves as though the world and its people are our adversaries. If you cannot get your way on a specific issue, consider letting it go. Act graciously and, if you cannot get your needs met, go to another source. Or just do nothing for a while and regroup. It is well said that when one door closes another one opens. A new door can come into view if we are not too busy trying to force the first one open. Put out effort, but don't *assume* it will be difficult. When you can let go of fighting to get the world to cooperate in exactly your way, things can happen easily. And so much more will.

EXPANDING YOUR VISION

There is much within our field of vision that we do not see. If we did see these things, our lives would immediately become more abundant by recognizing and enjoying things that are already there. If we learn to take pleasure in and appreciate these gifts, we not only add to our inner sense of prosperity, *we attract even more to us.*

The way in which we can instantly become more abundant is by seeing what is around us for our use and enjoyment. On the spot, we can enjoy nature and all its glory. We can phone a friend. We can enjoy a beverage, buy a magazine, take a walk. Taking so much in our lives for granted, we lose the sense of contentment and inner gratification these things can give us. This robs us of vital energy. We find ourselves reaching "far outside" to make ourselves feel better inside. Instead, we might look right around us and appreciate how little things add to the quality of our lives. By acknowledging what we already have, we can build upon it. It is well said, "Happiness is wanting what you already have." Though I do not agree with this statement entirely, it carries an important message. *Open your eyes and your mind to what you can experience positively today.*

In acknowledging resources already at your disposal, you increase the ability within you to see more opportunity and act upon it. I have yet to meet a single client who could not prosper more both financially and emotionally *from their present circumstances.* In some cases, I will not even go into a new plan of action with a client until we stop and acknowledge the abundant things they already have and how they might use or enjoy them. The client may not be using or appreciating what they have, but it does not mean it is not there. Allowing yourself to be prosperous begins with acknowledging and utilizing what is already there.

The Gratitude List

Spiritual and motivational leaders have long recognized the positive impact that can come from identifying and appreciating the positive aspects already existing in one's life. When a person formally takes pen and pad in hand to take stock in this way, it is commonly called making a Gratitude List. Creating such a list can be an invaluable tool for increasing your prosperity. Whether you make a list on paper (strongly recommended) or simply make a mental list, the goal is to recognize as many items as you can that add to the quality of your life right now, today. There is no item or aspect of your life too small to put on this list. It can include, but is hardly limited to, your gratitude and appreciation of:

individual possessions, friends, family members, office colleagues, professional resources, favorite TV shows, music, your home and individual aspects of your home, your talents, skills, personal qualities, someone's sense of humor, your neighborhood, the city or state you live in, the freedoms you enjoy by being in this culture, the technology you enjoy, books, telephone service, sunsets, sunrises, sunny weather, rainy weather, snow, breezes, animals, children, colors, lights, candles, holidays, weekends, your doctor or dentist, art, sports, freedom of religion, freedom of movement within your country, freedom to pursue your desires, highways, quiet roads, tall buildings, open fields, sexual pleasure, visual pleasure, delicious food, etc., etc., etc.

In making your list, be specific. You should have at least 50 items on your list that you are thankful for, appreciate and/or enjoy, or could, if you so desired. If reaching 50 was easy, go for 100. In doing this, the goal is to expand your vision and your appreciation of the abundance you now have. If you feel more positive internally, as well, so much the better. If you write it out, keep this list and look at it from time to time. Add to it as you follow these principles and enjoy greater success and satisfaction.

This exercise enhances the quality of your life through your perception RIGHT NOW. Even if you feel distressed or confused about your situation, you can stop, acknowledge, and make use of the blessings that are yours. Once you have this list, let yourself enjoy some of things on it. Keep this list handy. It might be especially useful when you feel down or frustrated, as you can forget, like all of us, how to help and motivate yourself. One simple reminder or action from this list can start your day over or enhance the quality of what you are already doing. Just as dwelling on what you do not have can keep you feeling frustrated and down, recognizing what you do have can lead the way to a better outlook and more satisfaction in your life.

CONFIDENCE AND COURAGE

You have already been introduced to the idea that communicating clearly appears as confidence to others. This happens as a by-product of being focused. We seem centered and certain of ourselves.

However, true confidence comes ONLY as a by-product of successful experiences. Confidence is not required before trying something new. On the contrary, it would almost be impossible to have confidence *before* going through new experiences. An *internal* feeling of security comes through the process of trial, error, persistence, adjustment of effort, and eventual triumph. This process is how we develop inner fortitude and the knowledge that we are capable in one or more particular endeavors. Therefore, let go of the notion that you "must be confident" as you begin to move ahead in new ways. You need only be willing to direct yourself to act (upon positive principles) and genuine confidence will come later because of your persistence and progress. Confidence in one area may aid you in trying something new, but you will not BE confident until you endeavor in a new area or develop a new skill with patience and consistency.

It will take courage, however, to act differently. If we allow ourselves to be more prosperous, we can expect to face fears that have kept us from maintaining and enjoying our "new successes." This accounts for the variety of reasons why we avoid abundant living. Our success may threaten and anger others. We may hurt the feelings of individuals as we take care of ourselves in an assertive manner. We may be criticized as we leave behind familiar habits. Many of us think we will face overwhelming responsibilities and pressure if we succeed. The idea of being prosperous may conjure up the thought that we will be alone without anyone to support us. Some of us project that we will feel enormously guilty enjoying our lives as others suffer and struggle as we once did. There may be countless reasons that keep us from letting ourselves prosper. One thing is certain: we must face the fear of being prosperous and challenge our projections of

Give Yourself a Raise

what will happen to us if we are.

Courage, like all qualities, can be developed. It will be easier to act with courage if we know there is no real danger in moving ahead. For almost all of us, taking new approaches and actions does not threaten our overall well-being. Decide to exercise courage and allow yourself to have more abundance.

A MATTER OF TRUST

Uncertainty will be with us all of our lives. A degree of uncertainty is a necessary part of good decision-making and choosing what is best for us. In this way, we ask questions that are meant to arrive at solutions. This is quite healthy. Remaining in uncertainty, however, when several viable alternatives are possible, is like a sinking anchor leading us to paralysis and despair. In reality, this is perfectionism masked as uncertainty. We want to make sure our actions will work out, and, therefore, keep questioning ourselves when we are really just afraid to change. We do not need to be certain things will work out. We may need, however, to adopt the belief that prosperity will come to us regardless of whether each individual decision or path we take ends well. The antidote, then, to destructive forms of uncertainty (perfection, procrastination, paralysis) is trust. Consider *acting* with trust.

Trust you can try something new and handle the results. Trust you can learn from attempting to move ahead. Trust you possess the same basic human resources and abilities as most of us, and that you can learn to adapt to new circumstances. Trust that if you are capable and intelligent enough to understand these principles, you are capable of growth and improvement with them. Trust you can be average, be imperfect, and be incredibly abundant. Trust you can begin by expanding your vision right now. Trust in your desire to be your best self, despite what obstacles and negative beliefs you may face. Trust that you can learn to stop depriving yourself and accept life's gifts. Act with trust that there is abundance within you longing to rise up and take form.

Most of all, trust you are not alone. In your noble efforts to improve your life and "let your own light shine" (as Nelson Mandela put it), you will meet others who will encourage you and support you toward your greater good. There may be those you leave behind, but there will be others ahead to greet you. I, too, am here in spirit with you. Your exciting journey is something to applaud.

Susan, 38, the co-owner of a small wholesale fashion accessories company, worked in partnership with two other individuals for more than ten years. Over time, Susan came to do all of the administrative work and analyzed and developed all new client accounts. Though she was responsible for more than 80% of the company's orders, Susan was only receiving a one-third share of the profits. Manually, she kept and maintained records of inventory, accounts, and company finances. She had one regular employee to help her with the tremendous additional responsibilities of ordering inventory, receiving merchandise, and packing and shipping orders. Her other two partners were, in actuality, sales representatives who were deriving partnership benefits for opening new accounts and generating only 20% of the company's revenues.

The company was doing fine, but my soon-to-be client was considering getting out of the business and contemplated leaving New York due to the overwhelming pressure she was experiencing. Her partners frequently complained of their work woes which created great resentment in Susan. They seemed to lack appreciation for the degree of her contributions. As a result of emotional stress, Susan developed severe back pain.

—◇◇◇—

Our first task involved getting Susan to partake of the prosperity that was already right there in front of her. She had been denying herself an equitable share of the business profits she generated. Her excessive sense of duty and responsibility was keeping her from confronting her partners. Her fear of their anger and rejection and guilt over the fact they would make less money if she took more profits kept her compliant and miserable. Eventually she became willing to accept the idea that she was depriving herself and could take action based on allowing herself to prosper. After several months of working together with me, Susan told her partners there needed to be a shift in compensation. In doing this, she became willing to bear the discomfort of their reactions. The partners did react. They were surprised, but they knew Susan's statements were well founded and something needed to be done to make sharing the profits more equitable.

As Susan became more adept at giving to herself, she let her resources go to work for her. During the course of the two years we have been working together, Susan is now receiving 65% of the company's profits, which is soon to be increased again. She has a staff of six regular employees and an additional four to six floaters during the busy season. Susan has moved the company into a space three times the size of her first office/stock room. She built herself a sound-proof office. For the first time ever, Susan has a private workspace. Now fully computerized (with 4 computers), the office runs sales, inventory, administrative, and financial records quite efficiently. The company's sales figures have increased more than 80% while cutting down her work hours. She has more than tripled her income.

In recognizing her true value to the business, Susan became the "lead" partner and the head of the company. At this time, her partners are still with the business, but are compensated according to their sales performance. Because the company's revenue has increased so much, her partners' shares did not drop substantially, while Susan's income increased dramatically.

Due to her efforts, Susan has added new clients, and company merchandise appears in over 200 new stores. She is beginning to spend more time with client development and merchandise display consulting -- the work she really enjoys. We are planning for her to hire a general manager and someday opening an additional satellite office. Susan never allowed herself to leave her office, even for lunch. Now, we are discussing sales and consulting trips around the country to meet with new and existing clients.

Susan has sought additional medical help and emotional support. This has greatly reduced her physical pain. Psychological counseling added a way for her to discover and fulfill her own needs. Though she still has difficulty spending money on herself at times, Susan has made tremendous strides in allowing more abundance into her business and personal life. Her stress level is continuing to decrease and is much better managed.

Learning to motivate and manage employees are other skills Susan is developing. Her future has unlimited potential for economic and personal growth.

Susan still works on allowing herself to be more prosperous. There are some old beliefs that get in her way, but there are riches in giving herself more time, energy, and money which she has allowed into her life. Susan's story is a clear example of how much more can come to us when we decide to face our fears and allow more abundance into our lives.

REMINDERS:

- More abundance exists for you right now, today. You only need to give yourself permission to let it in.

- Open your vision to what you already have right now. This adds to the quality of your life right now.

- You can make efforts, and you can let go of struggle and strain.

- Do not fight with others to get your needs met. Let go and extend yourself to new people and situations.

- It takes courage to try new things and let go. You have courage. Use it.

- Act as though you trust in yourself and eventually you will.

- Act as though you deserve prosperity and abundance and you will have them.

- Allow yourself to pursue things that will invigorate you, satisfy you and raise the quality of your life.

- Follow and practice the principles and ideas in this book that have inspired you. You will eventually feel you do deserve the best from life.

- Share with others what you learn.

SECTION III
ABUNDANCE SOUND BITES

What follows are suggestions regarding a variety of subjects from philosophical insights to handling money that are offered for your consideration. Several ideas are repeated from prior sections. These sound bites (short discussions) are meant to provide you with alternatives for addressing common issues as you travel the road to greater abundance and prosperity. If you disagree with any of these suggestions, move on to another subject. Then again, these ideas may give you a new twist on how to face an important issue.

The ideas listed here are approaches that have been practiced successfully by myself and my clients. These practical suggestions are not legal opinions. Where appropriate, before taking any action, check with a professional or other authority who can give you trustworthy advice or information.

MOVING FORWARD

Leave Your Comfort Zone in Increments
You will know when you are leaving your comfort zone by the level of your fear, anxiety, and resistance. Do not force yourself to move ahead too rapidly. To use a metaphor, start in the shallow end of the pool, work your way toward the middle, and over time, get into the deep end. If you experience a little anxiety and apprehension at taking a new action, that is fine. If your anxiety is intense, pull back a bit and try again another day. In this way, you will be able to leave your comfort zone and reach a new level of abundance naturally.

If you are having trouble taking action, you are possibly projecting too far ahead, or the actions you want to take are too emotionally frightening. To repeat again: break down your actions to the smallest possible step. Take a smaller step and then wait to take the next one. For example, if you are having trouble writing a letter, first, get the pen out. Later, get paper out. Later, just list the address on the sheet. Later, just put down the salutation: Dear ____. Later, write one paragraph. Finish a little at a time. Later, seal the letter. Later, send it. This may seem ridiculous, but it is not. *There is no such thing as an action too small to take!*

Keep Your Activity Level Moderate and Consistent
Practice taking actions and developing the quality of consistency. Approach things from a slow to moderate pace. We all need to learn to wean ourselves away from the Instant Gratification society we live in. The best way to assimilate positive change is over time. It is physically more beneficial to exercise twenty minutes each weekday than to exercise two hours each on Saturday and Sunday. Doing LESS consistently is MORE.

Take Action and Let the Results Unfold
If you water a flower, you do not need to stand over it to watch it grow. If you do this, you will only block the sunshine it needs. Take action and wait. Take another action and wait. It is a myth that being constantly productive is virtuous and character building. Many of us use this as a way to keep absurdly busy and avoid family, friends, feelings, and life itself. Being productive is healthy in moderation.

Give Yourself a Raise

In extremes, it is self-depriving -- not to mention exhausting. Once you begin to take action, give it time to work. You do not have to scurry around making sure all the seeds you plant will grow. Take a walk. Listen to some music. Take a nap. Let time pass. Things will happen while you do.

A client of mine, an insurance agent, would never leave his office for lunch or take a day off. He feared that if he did not constantly make sales calls, no business would come in. He conducted his home life just the same. Going from one thing to the next, non-stop. After a long period of coaxing, he finally agreed to take a lunch hour at least three days a week and scheduled a few days off during the course of the next month. He fell back into the habit of avoiding lunch hours, skipping a few. However, he still took his days off with much trepidation (with the admonition not to do chores, but to enjoy the day). He then proceeded to have his best month of the year. A lot of business came in through references (without any calls on his part). Also, he had a greater percentage of appointments through his own efforts. Could it be that he was not pushing prospective new clients as hard? Could it be that his tone and demeanor seemed less intense and desperate when he decided to act as though moderate effort was enough? Could it be that things could happen easily without all his machinations? His business is still doing better.

Don't hover over your own life. Give things time to work. Don't push. Keeping yourself extremely busy will give you dramatic effect but little genuine satisfaction.

Chop Wood and Carry Water

When you are having difficulty talking yourself into a course of action, forget about any of the reasons why you "should" do it. The Buddhists believe there is great power in simply completing tasks for their own sake. This has been described as "Chop Wood and Carry Water." Take each action for its own sake without focusing on outcomes. You are taking the action simply to enhance and strengthen your own inner spirit. The action, then, is all that there is -- a demonstration of your desire to strengthen your spirit through simple tasks. Some individuals even view this as a form of meditation. Taking actions as a demonstration of willingness to move ahead can motivate us when no logical or practical reason seems to get us going.

A friend of mine needed to move but could not get himself to look for a new apartment. His resistance was unbelievably strong. Knowing what I do for a living, he talked to me about it. I suggested he start making phone calls and asking others about vacant apartments based upon one simple promise I made to him. I told him that if he could just take two or three actions a day, something would change and he would be surprised by what it was. I told him he might not find an apartment and, besides, that was not the aim of the exercise. The only goal was to take these actions for the purpose of demonstrating willingness and building inner strength. That's it. Nothing else. This seemed odd, mysterious, and a little "airy-fairy" to him, but he became willing to give it a shot. My friend, being a little extreme, went off the deep end a bit and took more than 40 actions in two days. (Oh, well, one principle at a time.) He had absolutely no luck. He felt discouraged but better about himself for having done something. The next day he called me and told me something strange and wonderful happened. The night before, he was at a community service meeting and he was telling an acquaintance about all of his actions and his lack of "success." It seems another man overheard this conversation and questioned him about his need for an apartment. As it turned out, this other man was leaving the country for two years and needed to find someone to sublet his apartment immediately. My friend arranged to see the apartment, which was quite nice, and jumped at the chance. By taking action for its own sake, he changed. The rest happened as a by-product of his effort to change his attitude.

Chop Wood and Carry Water. It's not what you get. It's who you become.

PROSPERITY AND PEOPLE

Find Prosperity Partners

We all need to talk to others we can trust. Find those individuals who can be excited about your goals and make them your partners in prosperity. Share with them your actions, desires, accomplishments, disappointments, fears, and triumphs. They should be people who believe that any victory is great no matter how small. It could be a spouse or relative, but be aware that the best prosperity partners are usually those who have no vested interest in the outcome of your goals other than the joy of watching you grow. Do not go through your process alone. Professional therapists, business consultants, career counsellors, and motivational coaches, too, can be wonderful partners in your growth and success.

Broadcast Your Goals

Once you are clear about one or more of your goals, start to tell others of your plans and desires in normal conversation. People often naturally let you know of resources that may help you. This will also help you find partners for those goals. Obviously, do not share information that might come back to hurt you. Make it a practice, however, to keep expressing what you want without apology. This is a powerful way to positively reinforce and motivate yourself.

Hire Supportive and Competent Professionals

Accountants, attorneys, consultants, and the like might be very useful for you. Try to get references from friends. Also, ask for references from any professional you would consider using. Interview the person(s) even if they came through a reputable source. Listen to your instincts about them; do not judge by credentials alone. Be clear that you are getting help that feels "right." Remember, professionals work *for you*. You are the important person in the relationship. Therefore, you make the final decisions, and are responsible for actions you take, based upon their guidance. Do not turn your power over to them. If they are responsible people, their advice will be invaluable. Use it wisely.

If you do not have the money to use a professional on a regular basis, consider using their services on a less frequent basis. I work with some clients only once a month to keep the process and progress going rather than have them wait until they can afford to see me more frequently -- which would only delay their ability to live more abundantly. If I do my job well they will make progress (and more money) and eventually be able to see me more often. The same idea can work if you need an attorney, accountant, or other expert. Find someone who will help you on an intermittent basis, even if you only go to them once or twice in a year.

"Book-end" Your Actions with Someone

If a particular action is difficult for you, "book-end" it. This means that you talk to a supportive person *before* you take the action and then immediately *after* it is done. This can be a professional or personal acquaintance. You may want a number of people whom you can contact for this purpose. Then, if someone is not available you can find someone else who can support you. Keep calling until someone is available to speak with you.

It is a good idea to discuss a number of things on the "front side" of the book-end such as what you will say or how you feel about taking the action. You might ask the other person to role play with you (have a practice conversation) based on likely scenarios that could occur. You might discuss strategy or simply ask the other person for their perspective on the situation. Once you have discussed the action -- take it. On the "back side" of the book-end you report what you did and you might discuss what happened, how you felt about it, and what you may do next.

Book-ending can be extremely helpful in keeping yourself motivated -- not to mention the helpful hints and insights you might receive from others. In doing this, you also include others in your desire to move ahead. It helps you and it helps them. By doing so, we are sharing our goals, moving ahead in a positive manner, and endorsing our efforts.

Utilize Others as Invaluable Resources

You never know whom, or what, others might know. Relationships are a powerful resource in countless ways. Include others in your journey. Ask for their input and help. You do not need to follow up every lead, but there is a world of opportunity only one or two persons away from you. Always ask if you can use a name for a reference. Using names can make the difference between a shut door or a warm welcome. Once you meet new people, ask to use their names as well. There may be some who will decline, but as a principle, asking works.

Record the Names of People You Meet

As much as possible, anytime you make contact with anyone regarding a personal or professional task, write down their name for your records. If possible make a note or two about them so that you may recall your contact with them more readily. Refer to your notes upon contacting them again. Remembering peoples' names helps you reconnect with them and helps them treat you as a person. As a result, they are more likely to consider and grant your requests.

Put People Before Paper

Brochures, cover letters, resumes, promotional materials make a lot of people prosperous -- namely printers, copy shops, graphic designers, and writers. Not that this is bad, but do not let these pieces of paper come between you and the human connection. If you need to make a brochure, submit a proposal, write a letter, etc., do it only when necessary, clear, and obvious. There are exceptions, but in my experience they are extremely rare. Unless you derive income from writing, producing paper can be a tactic to delay yourself and turn over your power to an inanimate object. It is as though some of us want to avoid interacting with people to get ahead. We want the paper to convince them for us. Even when people request paper, ask to meet with them instead. Say to them, "Let me meet with you for a few minutes and then I can write something based on what I learn in our conversation." Or state, "I'm going to update my resume, but can I ask a little about the job right now?" (Then you can design your resume, if needed, for that job). This works. Try it. People. People. People.

Certainly, most of us will want to have a resume or information about our services available to others. But even so, I have had dozens of clients who have gotten jobs without resumes. I have been earning my full-time living as a consultant for several years and I do not have a brochure. If it becomes clear that I need one, I will do it.

If you need a piece of paper with information on it, keep it simple. The point is don't go out of your way to create promotional materials and other information on paper until you know you need it. Why kill a tree when you can make a phone call or request a meeting instead?

Develop Your Credentials from Where You Are Today

Credentials lend credibility. It's that simple. However, educational credentials, contrary to popular belief, are not as necessary as you might think. There are countless self-made men and women who had no credentials from established institutions as they began their rise to prosperity. You begin with organizations and names of individuals you have been associated with and you build upon them. One reference builds upon another. If you have the skills, training, and life experience to help others, do not let educational or institutional approval stand in your way. If you want to go back to school for genuine training, or to be licensed as required by law, fine. But do not do so to establish credentials. Before making this kind of commitment, see if you can use your time and money more creatively. Sometimes you only need to be associated with an individual, company, or institution in a single event or occurrence which can add to your credibility. Start where you are, use the names and experiences that you can draw upon now, and build upon them step by step.

CREDIT AND DEBT

Keep Your Debt Repayment to Creditors Below 10%

The rule of thumb is that you pay no more than 10% of your monthly net income to ALL of your creditors combined. (If you want to pay 10% of your *gross* income, do so only if you are not depriving yourself in any important financial area. Otherwise, you are reinforcing habits of deprivation and instant gratification which created the debt.)

If your minimum debt or credit card repayments exceed 10% of your net income, you are probably living beyond your means and may have problems with overspending or compulsive debt. If this is so, refer to the Resources section at the back of this book. In trying to pay off your creditors rapidly, you will almost certainly deprive yourself of money needed to lay a foundation for effective financial management and growth. Eradicating debts rapidly is a quick-fix that does not change the internal problems, habits with money, and self-deprivation that created the debt in the first place.

Pay Your Creditors *Something* Every Month

Do not avoid repaying your creditors because you do not have enough to make "appropriate" payments. If you can afford to pay only $10 a month to a total of ten creditors, do it. This is no joke.

The act of paying off your debts *consistently* is more important than how much you pay. If, because of your current reality, you need to send, literally, $1 or $2 a month to each of your creditors for a time, then do that. They will accept the money. Thus, the action of sending *something* every month is more important than the amount; because the principle of taking responsibility is the aim. Avoidance of our responsibilities creates negative feelings about ourselves. It is this habit we are breaking. The sense of esteem that comes from taking responsibility can enable you to be proactive and generate more revenue, which can then increase the amount of your debt repayments. To reiterate: quick fixes and pay offs do not change the internal problems and habits with money that created the debt. Acting responsibly, consistently over time, reverses the denial and avoidance that creates debt problems. The process of changing the core problem (avoidance and self-deprivation), not the symptom (excessive debt), takes time.

Beginning with payments of $1, $2, and $5 a month, I built a foundation of sound financial debt repayment. When my income increased, so did these payments. By doing this, as I stated previously in my story, 41 out of 44 debts have been settled. The remaining three will be settled using this same principle as well.

See Interest as Giving Yourself More Time

Do not be afraid of interest. Do not panic about paying high interest rates. When you increase your prosperity, you will increase your debt repayments. This will lower the principle and eventually the accumulating interest. If you can switch your debts to lower interest rates, do so. In any case, view interest as an investment in giving yourself more time. If you are getting socked with interest, you are probably living beyond your means or made a bad agreement. Seek professional advice. Again, there is no need to panic. If you practice principles of prosperity from this book and other sources, you can increase your income and your debts will eventually be paid off even if the interest is inflating your debts for the moment. It can be done and more easily than you think. If you can learn to refrain from acting impulsively, you will give yourself the time you need to reverse the patterns that get so many of us into trouble. It may take time, but full debt eradication is absolutely possible. As you become more methodical and consistent in your dealings with money, you can gain the necessary skills to negotiate or even eliminate the interest portion of some of your debts.

Use Credit Cards When You Have the Money, Not When You Don't

Lines of credit should be used almost exclusively for convenience, not credit. If you do not have the money to pay for an item in full today and your monthly payments are high and causing stress, you are setting yourself up for future financial hardship. Instant gratification often yields long-term deprivation and stress. Do not fall into this trap. Credit cards are like having fuel oil stored in your house. If you are careful and cautious, it may be useful to keep around. If not, there may be an explosion waiting to happen. Irresponsible use of credit cards is one of the most common ways that people live beyond their means and create financial crisis in their lives.

It is strongly suggested, if you charge something, you should shoot for paying off the entire balance when the bill comes in. If you are having money troubles, the axiom is: do not use a credit card unless you already have the money for the full purchase price set aside to pay the bill when it comes. Even if you do not have problems with credit cards, BEWARE. It takes very little to fall into the thinking "My credit is good. I can pay over time. I deserve to live well, so I'll let myself get this now." The problem is you can get this and that -- and that and that and that and that. *That* is when it can sneak up on you and make your financial life unmanageable.

Standardize Your Credit Card and Other Debt Repayments

Begin to send the same amount each month to your creditors as though you were making a standard rent or car payment. Remember, paying off debts is not a process of speed. It is a process of addressing money with simple guidelines in order to keep us from letting our emotional impulses create an erratic and chaotic financial life. If you begin to make more money, then increase the amount of your payments and keep that amount consistent for at least three months. Also, if less money is available, lower your payments for at least three months. Avoid sending different amounts from month to month. Consistency keeps your financial life simple. It instills confidence in the recipients of your payments when they see such stability in your methods. It stops you from depriving yourself of money you could spend abundantly on yourself rather than "get rid of" the debt.

I paid the same $15 a month to one creditor for more than 18 months. When more money flowed in, I increased it to $25 until the debt was paid. I could have paid this debt ($300 outstanding) in its entirety. Yet, I did not. I had already learned the hard lesson of keeping my cash flow high, increasing savings, and keeping my debt repayment moderate to very low. In the past, when I paid off balances lump sum and my back account was considerably lower, a sudden outstanding medical expense, repair bill, or other expense came up and I did not have the money to pay it because I rushed to pay off my creditors. This put me on the financial edge again. I learned the hard way to lower debt repayments for more than a year with some creditors until I could increase their payments again.

Do not act on the urge to get rid of debt. To work so hard to get rid of debts would be like having surgery to cut off excess body fat. It does not eliminate the underlying problem of overdoing that got you into trouble in the first place.

Simplicity and consistency are vital (and transforming) in dealing with money.

Consolidate Your Debt, If Possible
If you can, get one loan to pay off all your debts and maintain a **reasonable** monthly payment (approximately 10% of your net income). This is called consolidating your debt and it may be right for you. This is often done to lower the high interest rates some of us pay on loans and credit cards. Be careful of companies that offer consolidated loans at even higher rates than those you currently have. However, be aware that consolidation of debt will fail if you run up any more debt at all. If you can consolidate, it is vital then to commit to living only within your means. If that is difficult to do, then you need to increase your income before you even consider consolidating debts or taking on new debt repayments or expenses. Again, simplicity and consistency is the key.

Do not consolidate debt just for simplicity's sake. You may be able to negotiate with each creditor to lower your payments that, when totalled, would be less than your one monthly payment if you consolidated your debts. In other words, do not consolidate debt just to eliminate writing checks, contacting creditors and avoiding paper work. This would be avoiding responsibility for your finances and your life. At one point years ago, I was sending 13 small checks to creditors each and every month. This was time-consuming and difficult, but it eventually gave me a sense of self-discipline and self-esteem.

One of my clients owed more than $15,000 in credit card debt to eight different card companies; plus he owed on one bank loan. He wanted to consolidate his debt. With my help, this client arranged to borrow $15,000 from a relative and paid off each creditor. He cut up all but one credit card (to be used for convenience only) with the commitment not to use it except when he could pay off purchases in full *before* using it. His relative was to receive 8% interest annually. The client's debt repayment was 10% of his gross income which amounted to $250 a month. Without consolidation, his minimum payments had totalled almost $500 a month. I suggested that he make a printed payment schedule and give it to his relative, which he did. The client could have gone to a bank or mortgage company, but the interest rate would have been quite high and the minimum payment would have been much larger. At $250 a month, he will eventually pay off this debt.

For some of us, however, $250 a month would rob us of necessary living expenses. This is why debt consolidation is only a good idea under the right conditions. What if your monthly minimum payments are well above 10% of your gross income, and it would truly keep you on the edge to pay what is due? You need to come to the awareness that you have a problem (maybe even a compulsion) with money. If so, you will need to go through the painstaking process of learning to live your life differently with money -- as has been discussed throughout this section and this book. Like my client and myself, you will be committed to reversing a negative pattern of living which has probably developed over the course of adolescence and adulthood. If you falsely believe you have a "temporary problem," you may continue the cycle of financial pain and unmanageable living for years to come. It is the "underlying issues" of self-deprivation and impulsive living we are battling and working to reverse, not the "symptom" of debt.

Attempt to Lower Your Medical Debt

This is a difficult subject for many of us due to the skyrocketing cost of medical care. If the bulk of your debt is medical, try to negotiate or offer a long-term payment plan with no interest attached. If you are unemployed, you can apply for help from government services such as Medicare or Medicaid. If you cannot get assistance or a satisfactory agreement with medical creditors to help pay outstanding medical debt, treat this debt as any other debt -- to be paid slowly over time.

Maintain a Healthy Distance from Aggressive Creditors

In most states, there are laws against harassment by creditors. You can demand, in writing, that they only contact you by mail at an address you provide to them. If any company or person contacts you by phone after that, hang up politely (and quickly) and report them to the proper state agency, usually the Department of Consumer Affairs or the Attorney General's Office. Creditors are allowed to pursue you through the mail but cannot harangue you personally at home or work. If they continue to call you, YOU DO NOT HAVE TO SPEAK WITH THEM. Hang up. If they call again, hang up. Do not engage in conversation with abusive or aggressive people. Collection tactics are meant to intimidate you into sending them your money -- even if it means taking food off of your table. You need to take full responsibility for your debt and you can do so -- in writing. Tell them how much you are going to pay each month until your financial situation improves (no matter how small the amount), and do it.

You Will Survive a Bad Credit Rating

If you cannot or will not live within your means, your credit will be ruined at some point no matter what. Having a bad credit rating will not make you a social outcast. Buy yourself time to build a stronger foundation by slowly paying your creditors. If you get black marks against your credit, you can negotiate with your creditors to have them removed before you finally settle your debt. You do not need to even worry about your credit rating today unless you are making a major purchase that must be financed through a bank or other financial institution. However, if you find yourself in such a situation, it is unlikely that you are ready to make such a purchase without causing yourself hardship. (If you absolutely need to do so, like buy a car, you will need to lower your standards of what kind of car to get and be creative as to how you can pay for it. Otherwise, you will only prolong your poor credit habits and money problems.)

Remain calm. There is no debtors' prison. If you have a bad credit rating, you are one of millions of distinguished Americans who have the same problem -- some of whom make a great deal of money. Bad credit can be reversed over time. As you lower and eliminate your debts, you can work at ways to improve your credit history. You may want to go to a book store and buy a good book on cleaning up your credit rating -- but first things first.

Face Your Tax Debt

The most important thing to remember about outstanding tax debt is you must eventually "show up" and face the federal, state and local tax authorities squarely. The second most important thing to remember is tax departments are run by people, just like your friends, neighbors, and colleagues. Showing them respect, asking them for help and negotiating with them works. Continuing to avoid these issues works against you and is the most problematic way to deal with your taxes.

Make it a habit to file your current taxes even if you have no money to pay them. This is important to avoid accruing penalties and to establish a cooperative relationship with tax agencies. If you have not filed for any prior years, file your current taxes and then work backwards. For example, if you haven't filed 1988 through 1991, file 1991, then 1990, then 1989, then 1988. The government will eventually send you notices requesting payment for any taxes due. This is when you will need to address the money issues.

The most common problem associated with tax issues is failure to file in order to avoid facing the fact you cannot pay the taxes due. Do not fall into this trap. If you need to, consult with a professional (Certified Public Accountant or tax attorney) who can represent you in filing taxes, confronting tax problems, and negotiating with tax departments. To repeat: file your taxes and get a bill. The government's goal is to get you to make payments and eventually eradicate your debt. The reality is if you continue to avoid filing tax returns you increase the chances that tax representatives will be harder, less cooperative, and less flexible with you. If you avoid them and do not file all of your tax returns or make good faith payments, they will do whatever is necessary to get some money from you. Plus, after they attach bank accounts or personal property, you will still owe a balance if it does not cover your debt. This is why it is vital to proceed and take responsibility. Go slowly, but proceed.

Do not panic if you do not have money to pay your taxes in full. You may be able to work out a payment plan or be eligible for a tax deferment. You may even be able to make an Offer in Compromise to the IRS or your state tax department and pay five to thirty cents on the dollar (in a one time payment) to satisfy your entire tax debt.

Tax debt may need to be paid consistently and sanely over time, like all other debts. This can buy you time to ultimately increase your income and deal more effectively with the outstanding monies due. You should know, however, where other creditors may eventually forget about you and write your debt off as uncollectible, tax departments will always seek payment and eventually use legal means to enforce it.

In contacting and working with tax representatives, do not deal with someone who is harsh and threatening. You have the right to request to speak with or be assigned to another representative. Insist on dealing with individuals who treat you with respect. Remember, however, you must treat them the same way and not as adversaries who are out to hurt you.

After much urging from me, one client filed five years of back taxes and owed the IRS $47,000 (including penalties and interest). He sent them just $25.00 a month as a good faith payment toward this debt for more than 18 months. This $25.00 did not even come close to covering the interest each month. The point, however, is that he was showing up consistently and demonstrating to the IRS that he was taking responsibility. This allowed him some time to make them an Offer in Compromise for approximately 10% of his outstanding debt which they accepted as payment in full. Because he finally faced this responsibility, no legal actions were taken against him to seize bank accounts and property or garnish wages. Furthermore, he is committed to filing and paying his current taxes. He had been avoiding tax departments for ten years and it took nearly three years to straighten out his taxes and attain his current good status with them, but now he does not live in fear of the "tax man." His experiences with his tax debt taught him to treat himself and his other creditors with respect. He sends them standard monthly payments and he works toward increasing his financial prosperity which will eventually help him pay his total debt in its entirety.

Avoid Bankruptcy

In almost every instance that I have ever heard or experienced, bankruptcy does *not* give you a clean slate. In fact, it hurts your credit rating for years. More importantly, it does not "clean up" your overspending, underearning, or other poor money behaviors. (By the way, in some states bankruptcy does not rid you of responsibility for tax debt and student loans. The IRS may only let you declare a portion of your debt with them eligible for bankruptcy, if at all.)

Pay your debts off one-by-one. If they are overwhelming, you will need time to elevate your income, simplify how you handle your money and discover more creative solutions. To do so might take some of us years. To do this is not a test of character or strength. It is the most practical way to recondition yourself so that you can learn to live abundantly for the rest of your life. It is not the easy solution, but I believe it is the best one for 99.99% of us.

For almost everyone, declaring bankruptcy creates an internal stigma that we carry around inside ourselves. That is something we do not need when trying to present ourselves to the world as capable, valuable, and prosperous.

One of my clients was in the process of declaring bankruptcy when we began working together. He bought a summer house he could not afford and had the "bad luck" of not being able to sell it. He also ran up much debt through credit cards and a bank loan -- living well beyond his means. His wife of many years, who also had compulsive spending problems, was divorcing him, and since they had joint debt, they decided to declare bankruptcy to give each other a fresh start. This client worked with me only a short time. It was clear to me that dealing squarely with the issues of underearning, debting, compulsive spending, and money vagueness was extremely painful to him, as it is to most of us. Even after he declared bankruptcy, he was always in a money crisis and was continually living on the edge. At that point in his life, he was not willing or ready to face the issues that would release him from the problems he faced daily.

Bankruptcy, by its nature, is extreme which is contrary to

prosperous living. However, if you believe bankruptcy is the only way for you to get out from under your debt, then hire a competent professional to help you. Then, commit to getting counseling or other assistance to help with your money and debt problems. Focus on the underlying issues. Learn and practice better money management as outlined here and in other reference materials. Addressing your real problems is the ultimate solution.

Get Outside Assistance with Debt

In many localities and states there are non-profit organizations and agencies that help people in trouble with debt to pay them off. They can even negotiate with your creditors for you and get them off your back. Contact the Department of Consumer Affairs in your area or look in the phone book for these agencies. Try to use only non-profit agencies or groups; private companies may charge a handsome fee to help you. Be certain what type of organization you are considering. Using these agencies can be quite helpful. Be careful, however, not to confuse this practical help with facing underlying problems with debt, underearning, compulsive spending, or managing money ineffectively. If these are your issues, you can find yourself right back in trouble. Again, we want to go after the underlying issues, not only treat the symptoms.

It is strongly suggested you find a local Debtors Anonymous group (see Resources section) to help you. This national organization has helped individuals rebuild and transform their finances and their lives.

MONEY DYNAMICS

Without Fail, Save Money Regularly and Consistently

Putting money aside consistently for things you wish to purchase for yourself is vital to prosperous living. Every week or every paycheck, put a consistent amount of money away in two funds -- one in savings for purchases you wish to make, the other in a prudent reserve fund. You do this even if all you put in each fund is fifty cents a week. This is no joke. It is imperative that you take the action of putting *something* away consistently; the amounts are not what is important. Savings should not be used for necessities, only for things you wish to purchase that are abundant in nature. Your prudent reserve should never be used except, and unless, you are in dire financial straits. You can put away a specific dollar amount or a specific percentage of your income. You do this, no matter what, even if you have debt. If you are new to saving, and are able to financially, start out with $5 a week in each fund. If you need to, go down for a few weeks to $2 or less. I am quite serious. The principle is *consistency*, not amount. You can open your funds in two separate savings accounts, envelopes, cookie jars or under two separate mattresses. Just deposit the money *somewhere* that is set aside for only that purpose. You will find that amounts will naturally increase *if the habit is practiced*. Do not rush ahead with this either. Don't start dumping money into savings that you will have to yank out for living expenses. This defeats the purpose of saving. Over time, you will see your circumstances change by doing this.

Practice Having Money

Another reason for saving is the concept of HAVING MONEY. To foster and build the inner feeling that we are prosperous, we need to keep some money without spending it. If we spend all that we receive, the familiar feeling of living on the edge and never having enough gets reinforced.

Living on the edge is not a state of circumstances; it is a choice. This means when you leave the house, take more than enough money to make you feel abundant. Do not get down to carrying around your last dollar. If you do not let yourself have money in your possession, on your person, and in a prudent reserve, you will keep yourself from a feeling of internal abundance. If you spend money compulsively and cannot trust yourself, you may need to address this problem before you can be successful with this. Refer again to the Resources section in the back of this book. Overspending money creates feelings of scarcity and keeps us deprived. If we let ourselves have money in our possession, we add to the feelings of abundance that ultimately free us from financial hardship.

Spend Money in a Way That Makes You Feel Abundant

It is called a spending plan -- not a budget. A budget is constrictive, limiting and infers cutting back and depriving ourselves. A spending plan is proactive and lists all the things we need money for to live well in the world. This is more than semantics -- the words we use get reinforced internally and make a difference.

So, make a spending plan that is reasonable and attainable. Do not go beyond your spending plan impulsively. Chronic impulse or excessive purchases and expenditures are basically a way to deprive yourself of long-term abundance. If you are able to meet your basic needs easily, practice buying yourself quality items within your means. Get the better shampoo or name brand item. Buy a favorite magazine. Get more than one topping on that slice of pizza. Have coffee for a higher price at a finer restaurant or gourmet coffee bar. Practice spending a dollar more here and there to add to your quality of life. This is much better than an impulsive splurge on one item that robs you of day-to-day abundance. Spending abundantly, within your means, will easily turn into even more abundant, regular purchases once you move beyond the impulsiveness of "treating" yourself extravagantly. Treat yourself daily a little at a time. That builds inner prosperity. I have known people to walk two miles to save $1.25 bus fare and then go out that night and spent $80 treating themselves and a friend to dinner -- and then, two weeks later, they cannot pay the phone bill.

Get Help with Compulsive Spending

Compulsive spending and shopping are serious problems. They keep us in a perpetual state of deprivation and self-destruction. If you earn a decent income or have access to money and you are always out of money, living on the edge, or creating financial chaos, chances are you are a compulsive spender or shopper. Get help. Again, contact your local Debtors Anonymous group or get help from a professional counselor who understands these problems. This is no light or laughing matter. It can ruin the quality of your relationships and your life.

Do Not Hoard Your Money

There is a great difference between saving money, having money, and *hoarding* money. Hoarding money is the opposite of compulsive spending and happens when we deprive ourselves of quality living even though we have the money to improve our lifestyle. It is when we have the ability to pay our bills and then do not. Many years ago I had only $400 left in a bank account and had a phone bill of about

$50 that was due. I did not want to pay it. I was frightened that I might need that money for food. One of my mentors at the time told me, "Pay the bill. Don't hold onto the money." I gave him about fifteen objections to which he replied, "Don't hold onto the money." "What if I pay this and then run out of cash?" I desperately inquired. "Then," he said, "you will be in a position where necessity will make you get more money. Don't hold onto the money." Though extremely anxious, I did, in fact, pay the bill and my money did not run out. Out of necessity I took more income-producing actions.

Hoarding money deprives us just as much as compulsive spending. It says to ourselves and the world, "If I spend this money, I will have less and put myself in jeopardy. This money will not be replaced. So I will live in fear and suffer and stay in poverty thinking." Aside from your prudent reserve and allotted savings, don't hold onto your money. Pay your basic bills in a timely fashion. Give yourself vacations, medical treatment, better clothing, as long as you are spending your money abundantly, not compulsively.

Money needs to flow in order to grow. When you become more prosperous, it just flows in and out in larger amounts. Even if you are living "on the edge," do not hoard your money (holding on to it as though it is the last you will ever have). Depending upon your financial circumstances, this may be a difficult suggestion to follow because it means going against your fears. If you cannot do this alone or your situation is severe, get the support of others who manage their money effectively. At times, my expenses and income fluctuate. When the income is momentarily lower and the bills are higher, I can still get the old urge to hoard money to keep myself "safe." Now, however, I act in opposition to the false belief that there is not enough out there for me. Pay your bills with gratitude that you have the money. You will eventually triumph over fears that keep you in deprivation.

Treat Yourself First -- Then Others

It's the thought that counts, right? So, who do you think of first? Your own well-being or that of others? Generosity is great when it's not a smoke screen for self-deprivation. I know a woman who will spend $150 on a wedding gift (and she goes to ten weddings a year) and will not spend the money to get her nails done on a regular basis. She gives to others and deprives herself. The rule of thumb is treat

YOURSELF FIRST. Down the road, you can be more generous with money when you have so much you must share it to keep feeling good. Do this AFTER you have had experience treating yourself abundantly. If you are trying to keep up and impress others with gifts, so be it. Remember though, if you do it to your detriment, they will benefit and you will deprive yourself. Your needs come first. Your abundance comes first. Your well-being comes first. THEN share with others.

Commit to Making More Money

There is always a way to get paid more for your efforts. Even if you do not see how at the moment, you can still make it your business to make this true. You may need to change jobs, change cities, improve your skills, or improve your attitudes to do this. Take the risk to make more. It is scary to ask for more, but do not demand -- ask. There is no harm in that. If asking doesn't work in your current situation, determine that you will earn more money in another company or in some other way. As you know, there are others who get paid more doing some variation of the work you currently do. If they need to, these individuals move on to other professions or places that give them more abundance. Making more money is a choice. You are not trapped. Generating more revenue is absolutely possible if you have made it important for you to do so.

One of my clients took a new job where he knew he was being underpaid. I asked him to commit to making more money. He thought this meant looking for another job. Not necessarily. I asked him to look for opportunities to make more inside of his company. Within a few months, he believed he had found a way to increase his company's revenues. Before he offered his suggestion, he talked to one of the firm's partners. He made a proposal stating he could find a way to generate more revenue for the company. He asked for their agreement to give him a raise as an incentive, if his suggestions worked. Seeing the merit of this, they concurred. We discussed this for several more weeks and the client went in with his recommendations. His plans were implemented to a large degree and he got a 30% increase in his salary. This was small in comparison to the amount he brought to the company, but it helped him enormously.

If you decide that earning more is a necessity for you, necessity will become the mother of invention.

A DIFFERENT OUTLOOK

Adopt an Attitude of Service

We are either looking for others to be of service to us or provide service to them. So use this word, SERVICE, as part of your vocabulary. In looking for a job, you are trying to find a situation where you can be of SERVICE. In looking to hire a professional for your own purposes, you want someone who is motivated to provide conscientious SERVICE. Using your talents is being of service. Providing help to others is being of service. Asking others for help is asking them to be of service to you. Service is more than a word. It is a philosophy of grace and humility. An attitude of service eliminates the ego-centered aspect of seeking to move ahead. You may not do this perfectly, but when we *practice* this idea, it really changes the way the outer world reacts toward us. There is something transforming about giving of ourselves in service rather than making efforts to take as much as we can. Greed is self-absorbed and alienates others. Service is self-interested and, as a by-product, helpful to others. What goes around ... comes around.

Choose a Positive View

Do not apologize for who you are. Always present a positive view of what you assume others might think as a negative. You are not "too old for a new job" -- you have years of wisdom and experience. You are not "too young or inexperienced" -- you are eager to learn, highly trainable, and motivated to provide many years of service ahead. You are not "less desirable because you have been out of work for a year" -- you have had the luxury of not having to work so that you could become clear about the direction you want to take. You did not "fail in your last business venture" -- you started a company and learned an enormous amount about running your own business that will help you in future endeavors. Anything -- yes ANYTHING -- seemingly negative can be presented with an alternate positive view. In fact, *choosing the positive view is the truth.* The positive truth of the situation is always just as real and will be more compelling to those who eventually hire or interact with you. If you wish to take the negative view that some others hold, you are not living in reality. You are, in fact, hurting yourself by adopting the dark view of the facts of your life. Do not agree with possible detractors. The positive interpretation is more valid.

Visualize Success

Use your imagination to picture yourself as capable, confident, and moving forward in a poised manner. As you think of the goals and actions you are contemplating, you will naturally picture yourself in the situation and your mind will conjure up different scenarios, feelings, and outcomes. In visualizing success, you can start to see yourself as moving through these imagined situations naturally and effectively. You might want to find several quiet locations at home, work, or outdoors where you can be alone. Start by remaining motionless and just let your mind think of a situation that you would like to handle well. Even if you cannot seem to calm yourself totally, let your mind begin to picture you acting in a positive manner. Many people use visualization to specifically see themselves as successful in a particular scenario. There are many books on this subject, for example, <u>Creative Visualization</u>, by Shakti Gawain (see Resources section). Regardless of whether this is something you wish to learn as a discipline, you can certainly learn to take a few minutes, here and there, to let your imagination help move you toward a positive self-fulfilling prophecy.

Let Go of the Quick Fix

Quick fixes do not work. What is the rush? Where are you going in such a hurry? Do you think there will be no fear, pain, or frustration down the road? We cannot assimilate change through dramatic occurrences. In a study done about lottery winners, it showed that many of them depleted all their money soon after each yearly payment and often had to struggle to find more money toward the end of the year -- borrowing on next year's anticipated payment, for example. The money did not solve their internal conditioning of depriving themselves and living on the edge.

We are human. There will always be obstacles and both pleasurable and painful feelings. Getting something over with does not get the business of life over with. As they say, "No matter where you go, there you are." You cannot escape the fact that growth is a natural process, not a rapid advancement. For those who endeavor to improve themselves, all periods of rapid advancement are preceded and followed by long periods of slow growth. You can microwave a potato in ten minutes, but it takes weeks to grow it and years of experience by the farmer who had to learn to run his farm. Play the lottery for fun, but do not waste years of your life suffering as you try to reach the big hit with this or any other quick fix. You will get farther faster by building over time.

Take Personal Responsibility for Your Circumstances

If we are relatively well-adjusted adults, we are not victims. We may have been victimized in the past, but no longer. We may not be to blame for certain situations or attitudes that we are experiencing, but we are responsible for changing them. From a self-help book, there is a story of a mother who was confronted very angrily by her adult daughter about her shortcomings as a parent. The mother replied to her daughter that it was true many of the daughter's problems were caused by the mother and "have my name on them." The mother apologized for her parental shortcomings but then told her daughter that ALL the solutions to the daughter's problems "have your *own name* on them." These are wise words, indeed. All of us fall prey to feeling hurt, slighted, and unfairly treated. Do not fall into a victim mentality. Make living well your best revenge. Only you can be responsible for that.

Let Paradoxes Work for You

If you take an action and let go of the results, you have won twice. By letting go, your well- being is not attached to the outcome, and you have strengthened yourself through taking action. If the results are favorable, you have won yet again by demonstrating that good things can happen even when you do not need them to. Let go and you can have. Go slower, and you'll get there faster. When you need others approval less, you get it more. When good results are less important, you have more of them. These and other paradoxes work. Try to let go in all your endeavors. You will experience greater prosperity *and* peace in doing so.

Strive for Balance/Trust Your Instincts

Follow and trust your instincts -- even if it scares you. That goes for every important aspect of your life. Try to make choices of *balance* and consider going with the energy that seems most natural to you at the moment, regardless of whether it makes sense. Eat breakfast food for dinner. Take a nap at 7:30 pm. Spend time on something frivolous when you have serious work to do.

Go with your instincts. You will make mistakes, but you will learn over time how to listen more closely and trust them. Let choices come to you like a cool breeze that blows over your face. Get an image in your mind of something flowing, and imagine that you are going with it. I like to use the image of a river. I do not fight the current, nor do I speed ahead. I try to let it take me where it would naturally go. Use any image that comes to mind. Remind yourself to follow your instincts and let your natural energy take you. You do not need to know where it will eventually lead to enjoy the splendor of the journey.

Practice Making Progress

There is no way to get it all right. Life is a process of *practicing*. We may get good at something, and then the environment will change and we will have to learn and adapt again. Progress is enough. It is actually great. Don't we applaud an infant learning to walk a step or two? Then we do the insane thing of getting mad at them a couple of years later when they are not moving fast enough. This is what we do to others and ourselves. The triumph is in the effort you make. Easy does it, but do it. Keep practicing, and you'll get through it.

Pass Along What You Learn

The world is abundant. There is really enough for everyone. There are people dying from starvation all over the world, but scientists know for a fact that there is enough food for everyone. It is not *getting* to everyone. Make it your business to share the positive things you are receiving with others. Do not force your experience upon anyone. However, offer your thoughts openly and graciously. Withdraw if someone does not wish to, or cannot seem to listen. Still, as you meet others, naturally talk about what has worked for you. Doing so will only enrich you that much more. In this vein, consider donating regularly to charities, no matter what the amount. As you climb the ladder of success, reach a hand out now and then to help another person trying to climb beside you.

AFTERWARD

With all the courage possible, permit yourself to act upon these principles and enjoy the abundance you now see, and which will be coming to you. Do not let difficulties sway you from your goals. Be open enough to follow where abundance takes you.

Look to those ideas and information that might serve you well. Practice those ideas, to the best of your ability, that make sense to you. Remember to take your time, but keep practicing new approaches. Give them a persistent trial and you will see some exciting changes taking place.

By reading this book, you have attempted to open your mind to new ideas and learn how you may improve your professional and personal life. Congratulate yourself for this effort alone. It is indeed praiseworthy.

I thank you for taking the time to consider what has been presented here.

RESOURCES

ORGANIZATION

Debtors Anonymous
(self-help group, 12 Step program)
For information and meetings,
check local phone book listings or contact:

The General Service Board of Debtors Anonymous
P.O. Box 400
New York, New York 10163
Phone: (212) 642-8220

BOOKS

Mundis, Jerrold, How to Get Out of Debt, Stay Out of Debt and Live Prosperously, Published by Bantam Books, 1988 (ISBN 0-553-28396-0)

Laut, Phil, Money is My Friend, Published by Ballantine Books (as Ivy Books), 1989 (ISBN 0-8041-0534-0)

AGENCIES (to assist you with debt repayment and creditors)

Contact local or state Department of Consumer Affairs or the Attorney General's Office

In the New York metropolitan area contact:
Budget and Credit Counseling Services
55 Fifth Avenue
New York, New York
(212) 675-5070

Other Suggested Books and Forms of Psychological Support

There have been many individuals whose work has positively affected me. Their ideas and philosophies about human psychology, motivation, and spirituality can be great resources in shaping a positive outlook. I would heartily recommend the books, tapes, and works of the following people. Their unique perspectives may help bring you greater understanding of the challenges we all face.

Low, Dr. Abraham A., Psychiatrist - Founder of Recovery, Inc. (groups meet in U.S. & Canada), <u>Mental Health Through Will Training</u>, Published by Willett Publishing Co., Glencoe, Illinois
For a copy, contact: Recovery, Inc.
                              802 North Dearborn Street
                              Chicago, IL 60601
                              Phone: 312-337-5661

Gawain, Shakti, Lecturer and Motivational Teacher, <u>Creative Visualization</u>, Published by New World Library, San Rafael, California and <u>Living in the Light</u>, Published by Whatever Publishing, Inc., San Rafael, California

Hay, Louise, Lecturer, Healer and Motivational Writer, <u>You Can Heal Your Life</u>, Published by Hay House, Inc., Santa Monica, California

Bradshaw, John, Mental Health Lecturer and Counselor, <u>Healing the Shame That Binds You</u>, Published by Health Communications, Inc., Deerfield Beach, Florida

Bach, Richard, Writer of Fictional, Inspirational Novels, <u>Jonathan Livingston Seagul</u>, Published by Avon Books and Illusions: Confessions of a Reluctant Messiah, Published by Bantam/Doubleday Books

Also, the spiritual philosophies embodied in Twelve Step programs are great resources for study and growth. These programs are further recommended for those who suffer from nagging emotional problems, and/or compulsive behaviors, and have difficulty putting proactive ideas into effect. These kinds of chronic issues may need to be addressed before progress can be made.

Other forms of support may be available through friends, support groups, therapy, etc. The most important thing to remember is that you do not have to become a zealot or intense advocate for any group or person's philosophy. Be a magpie. Take a bit here and there -- whatever works for you. Take this piece and that, leave the rest, and weave your own colorful life tapestry.

MORE FROM THE AUTHOR

Individual Consultation, Speaking Engagements

An informative and thought provoking book can become an invaluable guide for any of us. Being inspired by what we have read, many of us will want to go further in implementing new approaches for ourselves and share our discoveries with friends, co-workers, and colleagues. If you are such a person, you may wish to contact the author of this book for information on individual consultation for yourself or your organization, or to speak at your professional association, school, community group, company, or business event.

If you are interested in inquiring about these services, please call:

Active Edit Publishing's 24-hour information line
212-439-5220

or send a fax to the author c/o Active Edit Publishing
212-769-9622

or you can E-mail the author at
ActiveEdit@aol.com

Your inquiry will be answered as soon as possible. If you are not available to receive a return phone call, let us know how to contact you.

Tell Us What You Think

The author of this book and ACTIVE EDIT PUBLISHING need your help to serve you better. Please tell us your thoughts on this book -- what was useful and what could be improved. Due to the wide-range of positive feedback received, the author is also considering creating a series of Essays (either written or on cassette tape) on these and other topics:

"The Psychology of a Resume and Cover Letter that Stand Out"
"Money Management for People Who Can't, Hate, or Don't Want to Do It"
"A Plan for Getting Clear About the Right Career for You"
"How to Deal with IRS and Other Tax Debts"
"Keeping Your Spirits Up During a Job Search"
"Basics Every Manager Should Know About Managing Employees More Effectively"
"How to Plan, Save and Spend for the Things You Want"
"Dealing with Difficult Personalities in Business"
"Increasing Your Company's Revenues By Improving Your Policies"

To contact us regarding these subjects or others, please mail, fax, or e-mail your complete name and address to Active Edit Publishing, Attn: Reader Feedback, 160 West 71st Street, Box 30, New York, NY 10023. We will keep you abreast of upcoming publications, tapes or services that are aimed at helping you become more prosperous and live more abundantly.

Purchasing Multiple Copies of <u>GIVE YOURSELF A RAISE</u>

If you wish to purchase five or more copies of this book for your school or organization, you can receive a discount by contacting us at the 24-hour number listed above. You may use your *Visa, MasterCard,* or *American Express* card for payment, as well as a check or money order.

ORDER FORM

To Obtain Copies of - **"GIVE YOURSELF A RAISE: Common Sense**
Principles To Help You Think, Act and Live More Abundantly"
VISIT YOUR FAVORITE BOOKSTORE; or order directly from ACTIVE EDIT PUBLISHING

Carefully tear out this page and use it for your order (or photocopy it),
or charge your purchase --
TOLL FREE 1-800-745-8874*

Please send _____ copies of <u>Give Yourself A Raise</u> at $14.95 per book   = $_____

Add $3.75 shipping for <u>each</u> book sent **via air mail**,

   7-10 *days* processing & delivery -- OR --

Add $2.25 shipping for <u>each</u> book sent **via ground delivery**,

   2-3 *weeks* processing & delivery   = $_____

                                                Subtotal   = $_____

Add sales tax (8.25% of subtotal) to orders shipped to a
New York State address or simply add --

   - $1.54 SALES TAX for <u>each</u> book sent **via air mail** -- OR --

   - $1.42 SALES TAX for <u>each</u> book sent **via ground delivery**   = $_____

                                          TOTAL**   = $_____

PAYMENT OPTIONS

Check one of the options below and with each order, please include your:
Full Name, Complete Address, Message Phone No.

☐ Personal Check or Money Order mailed with this form and shipping information to:
Active Edit Publishing, 160 West 71st Street, Box 30, New York, NY 10023

☐ Visa, MasterCard, Amex (Circle One)

  Card #_____ Expiration Date:_____

  Your Name exactly as it is on your Card:_____

  Your Signature:_____ Today's Date:_____

You can *TELEFAX* your Credit Card Order to Active Edit Publishing: 212-769-9622

Your Name: _____

Company:_____

Address: _____

City:_____ State:_____ Zip: _____

Telephone: (_____) _____ Fax No: (_____) _____

To speak with someone in person, call Active Edit's 24-hour information line at
212-439-5220. Leave a message and your call will be returned as soon as possible.

  * Residents of the New York Metropolitan Area -- Dial 212-439-5220 to charge your order.
** Materials ordered cannot be shipped without accurate payment. Express delivery can be provided
   for an additional charge. If for any reason you are not satisfied with your order, return it for a refund